The History of Gold

Crafted by Skriuwer

Copyright © 2024 by Skriuwer.

All rights reserved. No part of this book may be used or reproduced in any form whatsoever without written permission except in the case of brief quotations in critical articles or reviews.

For more information, contact : **kontakt@skriuwer.com** (www.skriuwer.com)

Table of Contents

1. The Origins of Gold
1.1 The Formation of Gold: Geological Processes
1.2 Ancient Gold Deposits: Where It All Began
1.3 The First Uses of Gold: From Tool to Treasure
1.4 Gold in Mythology and Early Religion
1.5 The Discovery of Gold in Ancient Civilizations

2. Gold in Ancient Civilizations
2.1 Gold in Ancient Egypt: The Pharaohs' Treasure
2.2 Gold in Mesopotamia: Trade and Wealth
2.3 Gold in the Indus Valley Civilization
2.4 Gold in Ancient China: From Currency to Art
2.5 The Spread of Gold Use Across the Ancient World

3. Gold in the Classical World
3.1 Gold in Ancient Greece: Myth and Reality
3.2 Gold in the Roman Empire: Wealth and Power
3.3 Gold in Ancient Persia: Kings and Conquests
3.4 Gold and the Silk Road: Trade Across Continents
3.5 Gold as a Symbol of Divinity and Power

4. The Middle Ages: Gold and Power
4.1 The Role of Gold in Medieval Europe
4.2 Gold in the Byzantine Empire: Continuity and Change
4.3 The Islamic Golden Age: Gold in Science and Trade
4.4 The African Gold Kingdoms: Mali and Ghana
4.5 Gold and the Crusades: Financing War and Religion

5. The Age of Exploration and Gold
5.1 The Gold of the New World: Conquistadors and Colonization
5.2 The Gold Rushes: California, Australia, and Beyond
5.3 The Impact of Gold on Indigenous Populations
5.4 The Role of Gold in Colonial Economies
5.5 Gold and the Slave Trade: An Unspoken Connection

6. Gold and the Development of Modern Economies
6.1 The Gold Standard: Birth of Modern Monetary Systems
6.2 Gold and Banking: The Rise of Financial Institutions
6.3 The Role of Gold in Industrialization
6.4 The Global Gold Trade: From Mines to Markets
6.5 The Shift Away from the Gold Standard

7. Gold in Art and Culture
7.1 Gold in Religious Art: Icons, Relics, and Rituals
7.2 The Use of Gold in Fine Art: From Ancient to Modern Times
7.3 The Use of Gold in Jewelry: Status and Fashion
7.4 Gold in Literature and Myth: The Allure of the Precious Metal
7.5 The Psychological Impact of Gold: Why We Value It

8. Gold in Science and Technology
8.1 The Chemistry of Gold: What Makes It Unique?
8.2 Gold in Medicine: Historical and Modern Uses
8.3 The Role of Gold in Electronics and Industry
8.4 Innovations in Gold Extraction and Refining
8.5 The Future of Gold in Emerging Technologies

9. Gold in Global Politics and Diplomacy
9.1 Gold as a Tool of Diplomacy: Historical Examples
9.2 Gold and War: Financing Conflict
9.3 Gold Reserves and National Security
9.4 The Politics of Gold Mining: Power, Corruption, and Control
9.5 International Gold Agreements: Cooperation and Conflict

10. The Environmental Impact of Gold Mining
10.1 The Ecological Footprint of Gold Mining
10.2 Case Studies in Environmental Degradation
10.3 Efforts to Make Gold Mining Sustainable
10.4 The Human Cost of Gold Mining: Health and Safety Concerns
10.5 The Future of Ethical Gold: Certification and Standards

11. The Economics of Gold
11.1 The Price of Gold: Historical Trends
11.2 Gold as an Investment: Safe Haven or Risky Bet?
11.3 The Role of Gold in Inflation and Deflation
11.4 Gold and Currency Fluctuations
11.5 The Future of Gold in Global Finance

12. Gold and Society: Wealth and Inequality
12.1 Gold and Social Stratification: Historical Perspectives
12.2 The Role of Gold in Symbolizing Wealth
12.3 Gold and Poverty: The Paradoxes of Wealth
12.4 The Ethics of Gold Ownership: Hoarding vs. Sharing
12.5 Gold and Global Inequality: Bridging the Gap

13. Gold in Modern Culture
13.1 Gold in Fashion: The Ultimate Status Symbol
13.2 Gold in Music and Entertainment: From Bling to Lyrics
13.3 Gold in Sports: Trophies, Medals, and Glory
13.4 The Representation of Gold in Film and Media
13.5 The Psychological Appeal of Gold Today

14. Gold and Technology: Past, Present, Future
14.1 Gold in Ancient Technology: Early Innovations
14.2 Gold in Modern Electronics: Essential and Irreplaceable
14.3 The Future of Gold in Nanotechnology
14.4 Innovations in Gold Recycling: A Sustainable Future
14.5 The Potential for Gold in Renewable Energy

15. Gold and the Future of Money
15.1 The Debate Over Returning to the Gold Standard
15.2 Cryptocurrency vs. Gold: The New Digital Gold Rush?
15.3 The Role of Gold in a Cashless Society
15.4 The Global Shift Toward Digital Gold
15.5 Gold as a Universal Currency: A Timeless Standard?

16. The Myths and Legends of Gold
16.1 The Myth of El Dorado: The City of Gold
16.2 The Philosopher's Stone: Alchemy and Gold
16.3 Gold in Ancient Folklore: Tales of Wealth and Woe
16.4 The Curse of the Pharaohs: The Dark Side of Gold
16.5 Modern Myths: Gold Heists and Lost Treasures

17. The Future of Gold Exploration
17.1 The Search for New Gold Deposits
17.2 Technological Advances in Gold Prospecting
17.3 The Role of Artificial Intelligence in Gold Mining
17.4 Gold from Space: Asteroid Mining and Beyond
17.5 Sustainable Gold Mining: The Next Frontier

18. Gold in Global Trade and Economics
18.1 Gold as a Global Commodity: Trade and Exchange
18.2 The Impact of Gold on National Economies
18.3 Gold and International Relations: A Historical Perspective
18.4 The Role of Gold in Modern Economic Crises
18.5 The Future of Gold in the Global Economy

19. The Environmental Future of Gold
19.1 Addressing the Environmental Impact of Gold Mining
19.2 Innovations in Eco-Friendly Gold Extraction
19.3 The Role of Governments in Regulating Gold Mining
19.4 Gold Recycling: The Environmental Benefits
19.5 Community-Led Mining Initiatives: A Sustainable Approach

20. Conclusion: The Enduring Legacy of Gold
20.1 Gold's Role in Human History: A Summary
20.2 The Cultural and Economic Significance of Gold
20.3 Gold and Human Identity: Wealth, Power, and Perception
20.4 The Future of Gold in the 21st Century
20.5 Final Thoughts: The Timeless Allure of Gold

Chapter 1

The Origins of Weaponry

The Formation of Gold

Gold is a precious metal that has captivated human imagination for millennia, but its formation is a complex geological process that occurs over millions of years beneath the Earth's surface. Understanding how gold forms requires a grasp of several geological phenomena, including the processes of nucleosynthesis, hydrothermal activity, and sedimentation.

Nucleosynthesis: The Cosmic Origins of Gold

The story of gold begins far beyond the Earth, in the heart of stars. Gold is formed through a process called nucleosynthesis, which occurs during supernova explosions—massive stellar detonations that happen at the end of a star's life cycle. During these explosive events, heavy elements are forged from lighter ones in a series of nuclear reactions. Specifically, gold is formed from the rapid neutron capture process, known as the r-process. When these stars explode, they scatter gold and other heavy elements across the cosmos, where they eventually coalesce into new celestial bodies, including our planet.

Geological Processes: From Stars to Earth

Once gold-containing materials find their way to Earth, geological processes take over. The young Earth was initially a molten mass, and as it cooled, dense metals like gold sank toward the core while lighter elements formed the crust. Over geological timescales, tectonic activity, volcanic eruptions, and erosion would reshape the Earth's surface, leading to the concentration and deposition of gold in various forms.

Gold is most commonly found in two geological environments

1. Primary Deposits: These deposits are formed through hydrothermal processes, where hot, mineral-rich water circulates through cracks and fissures in the Earth's crust. As this hot water cools, it precipitates minerals, including gold, which can accumulate in veins and lodes. Often found in mountainous regions or near tectonic plate boundaries, these deposits are typically mined through hard rock mining techniques.

2. Secondary Deposits: Over time, primary deposits can be subjected to weathering and erosion. The gold contained in these deposits can be liberated from the surrounding rock and transported by water. This process leads to the formation of alluvial deposits, which are found in riverbeds and floodplains. These secondary deposits are usually easier to mine and have historically been the target of placer mining methods, where gold is extracted from sediments using water and gravity separation techniques.

The Role of Geochemistry

The formation of gold is also influenced by geochemical factors, including the presence of specific minerals and the pH levels of the surrounding environment. Gold is often found alongside other minerals, such as quartz, pyrite, and sulfides. These minerals can influence the solubility and transport of gold within hydrothermal fluids. Additionally, the temperature and pressure conditions in the Earth's crust play a critical role in determining how and where gold deposits are formed.

Geological Timeframes

The formation of gold deposits is not a rapid process; it takes millions of years for significant concentrations to develop. Factors such as tectonic movements, volcanic activity, and erosion continuously reshape the Earth, leading to the formation of new gold deposits while weathering away others.

In summary, the geological processes that form gold are intricate and multifaceted, involving cosmic events, tectonic activities, hydrothermal systems, and the interplay of various geochemical conditions. Understanding these processes not only sheds light on the origin of gold but also provides valuable insights into the mining and economic significance of this treasured metal throughout human history. Gold's journey from the heart of a star to the depths of the Earth culminates in its eventual discovery and utilization by humankind, underscoring its timeless allure and enduring legacy.

Ancient Gold Deposits

Gold, often revered as the "king of metals," has been a part of human civilization since its inception. Its captivating luster and rarity made it a sought-after resource, prompting early humans to seek out its sources in the Earth's crust. The origins of gold deposits trace back to geological processes that occurred millions of years ago, shaping the landscape and creating the foundations for future human interaction with this precious metal.

Geological Formation of Gold

The formation of gold in the Earth's crust is primarily attributed to hydrothermal processes, which involve the movement of hot, mineral-rich water through rock formations. These processes often occur in areas with volcanic activity, where the intense heat causes the dissolution of gold from surrounding rocks. As this mineral-rich water cools, the gold precipitates out, often forming veins within the host rock. Other significant processes include the weathering and erosion of gold-bearing rocks, which can lead to the deposition of gold in alluvial deposits—gravel beds where gold accumulates as sediments are washed away.

In prehistoric times, the earliest gold deposits were likely found in riverbeds and streams, where the natural forces of erosion concentrated the metal. These alluvial deposits were more accessible to early humans, who could easily collect gold flakes and nuggets washed down from higher elevations. The simplicity of this collection method made gold an attractive resource for primitive societies.

Early Sources of Gold

The earliest known use of gold dates back to around 4000 BCE in regions such as the Middle East, particularly in the areas that would become known as Egypt and Mesopotamia. Archaeological evidence suggests that gold was being mined from alluvial deposits in the Nile River and its tributaries, as well as from gravel beds in the region. The ancient Egyptians, for instance, established some of the first gold mining operations, utilizing primitive tools to extract gold from the riverbeds and nearby hills.

In addition to Egypt, other regions such as the Caucasus and parts of Sub-Saharan Africa also became known for their gold deposits. The Varna Necropolis in Bulgaria, dating back to around 4600 BCE, revealed some of the oldest known gold artifacts, indicating that these early societies not only collected gold but also fashioned it into decorative items. This suggests a cultural significance attached to gold, beyond mere economic value.

Cultural Significance and Early Uses

The allure of gold was not limited to its physical properties. Early humans ascribed spiritual and cultural significance to gold, associating it with the divine and the immortal. In many ancient cultures, gold was seen as a symbol of wealth, power, and status. In Egypt, it was often placed in tombs as offerings to the gods and as a means to ensure a safe passage to the afterlife. The use of gold for decorative purposes, such as jewelry and ceremonial artifacts, reflects its importance in social and religious contexts.

The discovery and utilization of gold in prehistoric times marked a pivotal moment in human history. It laid the groundwork for complex societies, trade networks, and cultural exchanges. As civilizations advanced, the methods of gold extraction and processing became more sophisticated, leading to the establishment of mining communities and the rise of economies centered around this precious metal.

Conclusion

In summary, the ancient gold deposits laid the foundation for humanity's enduring relationship with gold. From its geological formation to its early extraction and cultural significance, gold has transcended its role as a mere metal, evolving into a symbol of human aspiration and achievement. As we delve into the historical narrative of gold, we uncover not just the evolution of a material, but the story of humanity itself, intertwined with the quest for beauty, power, and immortality.

The First Uses of Gold: From Tool to Treasure

Gold, with its distinctive luster, malleability, and resistance to tarnish, has captivated humans for millennia. Its unique properties made it one of the first metals to be used by early civilizations, transitioning from a practical resource to a symbol of wealth and power. This section explores the multifaceted roles that gold played in the lives of early humans, focusing on its initial uses, the technological innovations it inspired, and its evolution into a treasured commodity.

Practical Uses of Gold

The earliest uses of gold can be traced back to prehistoric times, when it was likely discovered in its native form in riverbeds and on hillsides. Due to its softness, gold was easy to work with, allowing early humans to shape it into rudimentary tools and ornaments. While the specific tools made from gold in those early days are difficult to pinpoint, it is likely that gold was initially used for decorative purposes rather than functional ones. The first artifacts—such as simple beads and pendants—were created to adorn the human body, indicating that even in prehistoric societies, aesthetics played a significant role in daily life.

Cultural Significance

As societies evolved, so did the significance attributed to gold. It began to represent more than just a physical object; it became a cultural and spiritual symbol. Ancient cultures viewed gold as a divine material. For instance, in ancient Egypt, gold was associated with the gods and the afterlife, leading to its use in burial artifacts and ceremonial items. The famous burial mask of Pharaoh Tutankhamun, made of gold, exemplifies how gold transitioned from merely a decorative element to a powerful symbol of status and divinity.

The Advent of Goldsmithing

By around 4000 BCE, the art of goldsmithing began to emerge. This development marked a significant technological innovation, as skilled artisans learned to manipulate gold into intricate designs. The techniques of alloying, hammering, and casting allowed for the creation of more complex jewelry and artifacts, enhancing gold's desirability. These advancements not only showcased human ingenuity but also set the stage for gold to transition from a simple metal to a medium of exchange and status.

Gold as Currency

As trade networks expanded, the need for standardized currency became apparent. Gold's rarity, durability, and divisibility made it an ideal candidate for a medium of exchange. The first gold coins are believed to have been minted in the kingdom of Lydia around 600 BCE, marking a revolutionary shift in economic systems. With the introduction of currency, gold became a tool of commerce, facilitating trade and economic growth across ancient civilizations.

Symbol of Wealth and Power

Gold's natural allure and its association with prosperity solidified its role as a symbol of wealth and power. Rulers and elites adorned themselves with gold jewelry and used gold to display their status. The accumulation of gold became a means of asserting dominance and securing political power. In many cultures, large quantities of gold were hoarded and displayed in temples or palaces, further intertwining the metal with both divine and earthly authority.

Conclusion

From its early days as a decorative element to its emergence as a cornerstone of trade and wealth, gold has played an integral role in human history. Its early uses laid the foundation for the complex socio-economic systems we see today. As a material that represents beauty, power, and value, gold continues to capture the human imagination, reminding us of our enduring fascination with this precious metal. Ultimately, the journey of gold from tool to treasure reflects not only technological and artistic advancements but also the deep-seated human desire for beauty, status, and security.

Gold in Mythology and Early Religion

Gold has long held a revered place in human culture, transcending its physical properties to become a symbol of divinity, power, and the supernatural. In ancient societies, the allure of gold was not merely due to its lustrous appearance and malleability but was deeply intertwined with spiritual beliefs and religious practices. This section delves into the multifaceted roles that gold played in mythology and early religion across various ancient cultures, illustrating its significance as a sacred metal.

In many ancient civilizations, gold was considered a manifestation of divine qualities. The Egyptians, for instance, associated gold with the sun god Ra, believing it to be the flesh of the gods. This divine connection made gold an essential material in funerary practices and temple construction. The tombs of pharaohs were adorned with gold artifacts, which were thought to accompany the deceased in the afterlife, ensuring their immortality and favor with the gods. The lavish burial of Tutankhamun is a prime example, showcasing not only the wealth of the young pharaoh but also the spiritual beliefs surrounding gold's protective and life-giving properties.

In Mesopotamia, gold was equally venerated. The Sumerians and later the Babylonians used gold in religious iconography, creating intricate idols and artifacts that adorned temples dedicated to their pantheon of gods. Gold's durability and rarity symbolized the eternal nature of the divine, making it a suitable medium for offerings and sacred objects. The famous Ishtar Gate of Babylon, embellished with gold and lapis lazuli, reflected the city's grandeur and its commitment to worshiping the goddess Ishtar, the embodiment of love and war.

The significance of gold extended to the Indus Valley Civilization, where archaeological finds suggest its use in crafting jewelry and ritual objects. Gold was likely not just a marker of wealth but also a means of connecting with the divine. The intricate designs of gold jewelry found in sites like Mohenjo-Daro indicate a cultural appreciation for beauty, which may have been perceived as a reflection of the divine order in the universe.

In ancient Greece, gold was imbued with mythological significance, often appearing in tales of gods and heroes. The Greek god Hermes, the messenger of the gods, was often depicted with gold, symbolizing wealth and abundance. The myth of King Midas, who could turn everything he touched into gold, serves as a cautionary tale about the dangers of greed and the desire for wealth. This duality reflects the complexity of gold's role in human desire and moral lessons, showcasing how it could represent both blessings and curses.

Furthermore, in the spiritual practices of ancient China, gold was seen as a symbol of purity and perfection. It was used in rituals and as a medium for offerings to ancestors, reinforcing the cultural belief in the interconnection between the living and the spiritual realm. The Chinese emperors would often wear gold to signify their divine right to rule, establishing a direct link between gold, authority, and the heavens.

The spiritual significance of gold in ancient cultures also manifested in its use as a currency for trade and offerings. Gold coins were often minted with images of deities or symbols of power, reinforcing the belief that wealth and divine favor were intertwined. This practice established a lasting legacy, as gold continued to be a standard for economic transactions, rooted in its sacred connotations.

In conclusion, gold's role in mythology and early religion highlights its enduring impact on human civilization. As a symbol of divine power, immortality, and wealth, gold transcended mere material value, becoming a vital element in the spiritual fabric of ancient cultures. Its multifaceted significance continues to resonate, reflecting humanity's ongoing quest for meaning, connection, and transcendence.

The Discovery of Gold in Ancient Civilizations

The allure of gold has captivated humanity since its earliest days, and its discovery marked a significant turning point in the development of ancient civilizations. This precious metal, with its lustrous sheen and malleability, was more than just a commodity; it represented power, wealth, and divinity. The emergence of gold as a valuable resource can be traced back to several ancient societies, each contributing to the understanding and utilization of this remarkable metal.

Early Discoveries

The earliest known use of gold dates back to around 4,600 years ago, with archaeological evidence suggesting that the ancient Egyptians were among the first to mine and refine it. Gold was often found in its natural state in riverbeds and alluvial deposits, making it relatively easy for early humans to collect. The Egyptians, particularly, began to recognize its value not just as a decorative item but also as a symbol of status and power. This recognition laid the groundwork for the extensive gold mining and craftsmanship that would define their civilization.

In Mesopotamia, another cradle of civilization, gold was discovered through similar processes. Archaeological sites in what is now Iraq have shown evidence of gold ornaments dating back to the Sumerians around 3,000 BCE. The Sumerians utilized gold for various purposes, including jewelry, religious artifacts, and as a medium of exchange in trade. The presence of gold in these early societies reflects not only their technological advancements in metallurgy but also their burgeoning social hierarchies, where wealth accumulation became a marker of status.

Utilization in Society

As civilizations progressed, the use of gold expanded in complexity and significance. The Egyptians, for example, utilized gold extensively in their burial practices, believing it to be a symbol of eternal life. The famous burial mask of Pharaoh Tutankhamun, crafted from gold, exemplifies the intricate artistry and importance of gold in religious and cultural contexts. Gold was also used to create elaborate tombs and monuments, reinforcing the belief that the afterlife was a continuation of earthly existence where wealth and beauty were paramount.

In the Indus Valley Civilization, which thrived around 2500 BCE, gold was used to create seals and personal ornaments that indicated wealth and power. The use of gold in trade also began to emerge, as the Indus Valley merchants exchanged gold goods with neighboring regions, integrating gold into their economic systems.

Gold's Role in Trade and Diplomacy

The discovery of gold also had profound implications for trade and diplomacy among ancient civilizations. It served as a standard of wealth and facilitated trade relations between cultures. For instance, the Phoenicians, renowned traders of the ancient world, utilized gold as a key medium for commerce, enabling them to establish a vast trading network across the Mediterranean.

The political significance of gold cannot be overstated. Rulers and elites used gold not just as a means of wealth but as a tool to solidify power and influence. The Achaemenid Empire of Persia, for example, capitalized on its vast gold resources to fund military campaigns and expand its territory, showcasing the link between gold and imperial ambition.

Conclusion

In summary, the discovery of gold in ancient civilizations was not merely an accident of geology; it was a catalyst for cultural and economic development. The ways in which early societies harnessed gold reflect their values, beliefs, and aspirations. From its role in religious practices to its significance in trade and politics, gold has woven itself into the very fabric of human civilization. Its enduring allure continues to resonate through the ages, shaping the course of history in ways that are as profound as they are multifaceted.

Chapter 2

Gold in Ancient Civilizations

Gold in Ancient Egypt

Gold has held a significant place in the culture and economy of Ancient Egypt, epitomizing wealth, power, and divine favor. The Egyptians' relationship with gold was multifaceted, incorporating its use in rituals, burial practices, art, and currency, thereby solidifying its status as a symbol of the divine and earthly authority.

Mining and Extraction

The quest for gold in Ancient Egypt dates back to the Predynastic period, around 4000 BCE, when the earliest known gold artifacts were created. Egypt was rich in natural resources, particularly in the Eastern Desert and Nubia, areas that were home to considerable gold deposits. Egyptian miners utilized simple yet effective techniques such as panning for gold in riverbeds and using fire to break up ore. They would heat the rock to a high temperature, causing it to crack and become more manageable for extraction.

Mining expeditions were often organized by the state, reflecting the centralized power of the Pharaohs. Workers, including skilled laborers and slaves, were deployed to these mines, and the labor was often harsh. The labor force was organized into teams, each with specific tasks, ranging from the extraction of gold to processing and refining it. The mined gold was typically melted and cast into ingots or used to create jewelry and other artifacts.

Symbolism and Ritual Use

Gold was not merely a metal to the Egyptians; it was imbued with profound spiritual significance. The color itself was often associated with the gods and the afterlife. The Egyptians believed gold could confer immortality, as seen in their burial practices. Pharaohs were often interred with vast quantities of gold, including elaborate tombs filled with gold jewelry, masks, and ceremonial items. The most famous of these is the burial mask of Tutankhamun, which is a masterpiece of craftsmanship and a testament to the importance of gold in funerary rites.

Gold was also used in religious contexts, with temples often adorned with gold leaf and gilded statues of deities. The use of gold in sacred spaces reinforced its connection to the divine, as it was believed to reflect the light of the sun god Ra, symbolizing purity and eternal life.

Economic Role

In addition to its religious and symbolic significance, gold played a crucial role in the economy of Ancient Egypt. It served as a medium of exchange, especially in trade with neighboring regions. The Egyptians engaged in extensive trade networks that extended to the Levant, Nubia, and beyond, where gold was a valuable commodity. In this context, gold was often exchanged for luxury goods, raw materials, and other resources.

The centralized nature of the Egyptian state also meant that the Pharaohs had control over gold production and distribution. This control reinforced their authority and allowed them to finance monumental projects, such as the construction of temples and pyramids, which were often adorned with gold decorations.

Conclusion

Gold in Ancient Egypt was much more than a precious metal; it was a symbol of power, divinity, and wealth that permeated every aspect of society. From the arduous processes of mining and refining to its use in religious ceremonies and economic transactions, gold was woven into the very fabric of Egyptian culture. The legacy of gold in Ancient Egypt continues to captivate modern audiences, reflected in the grandeur of its artifacts and the enduring fascination with its role in one of history's most remarkable civilizations.

Gold in Mesopotamia: Trade and Wealth

Mesopotamia, often heralded as the cradle of civilization, was a region where the emergence of urban centers, trade networks, and cultural advancements fundamentally reshaped human history. Situated between the Tigris and Euphrates rivers, this fertile land was rich in resources, including the coveted metal gold, which played a pivotal role in the economic and cultural life of its societies.

Gold in Mesopotamia was not merely a decorative item; it represented wealth, power, and status. The earliest evidence of gold artifacts in this region dates back to the late Neolithic period, but it was during the Bronze Age that the use of gold became deeply integrated into daily life and commerce. Goldsmiths emerged as skilled artisans, capable of crafting intricate jewelry, ceremonial objects, and utilitarian items that showcased the metal's luster and malleability. These artisans were essential to the economic structure, providing both luxury goods for the elite and more practical applications for common people.

Trade was a cornerstone of Mesopotamian society, facilitated by the region's strategic location at the crossroads of various cultures. Gold was a highly sought-after commodity, often traded alongside silver, textiles, and agricultural products. The city-states of Mesopotamia, such as Ur,

Babylon, and Akkad, engaged in extensive trade networks that extended to neighboring regions, including the Indus Valley and Egypt. Notably, the Sumerians developed one of the world's first known systems of writing, cuneiform, which was utilized for record-keeping in commercial transactions. Clay tablets from this era reveal detailed accounts of gold trade, including the quantities exchanged and the parties involved, underscoring its significance in the economy.

The use of gold as a medium of exchange was also prevalent. While barter was common, gold's intrinsic value allowed it to function as a form of currency, facilitating trade and commerce. Gold's rarity and desirability made it a reliable measure of wealth and a means of storing value. Merchants and traders often used gold to settle debts and conduct transactions, reinforcing its role as a critical component of the Mesopotamian economy.

In addition to its economic implications, gold held significant cultural and religious importance. The Mesopotamians believed that gold was associated with the divine, symbolizing purity and immortality. Temples dedicated to various deities were adorned with gold ornaments, and priests often wore gold jewelry as a testament to their status and connection to the divine. The famous Ishtar Gate of Babylon, embellished with gold and lapis lazuli, exemplified the city's wealth and the reverence for the gods.

Moreover, the accumulation of gold was often tied to the concept of kingship. Rulers displayed their power and authority through lavish displays of gold, both in personal adornments and in monumental architecture. Gold became a symbol of political authority, with kings often depicted wearing gold regalia in art and literature. This connection between gold and power further entrenched its value within the society.

In conclusion, gold in Mesopotamia was far more than a mere metal; it was a cornerstone of trade and wealth that shaped the region's economy, culture, and politics. Its utilization in commerce and as a symbol of divine favor and royal authority illustrates the multifaceted roles that gold played in one of history's most influential civilizations. As Mesopotamia laid the foundations of urban society, the legacy of gold as a medium of exchange and a marker of status has endured through the ages, continuing to influence societies long after the fall of its ancient city-states.

Gold in the Indus Valley Civilization

The Indus Valley Civilization, flourishing from approximately 3300 to 1300 BCE, is one of the world's earliest urban cultures, notable for its advanced city planning, sophisticated drainage systems, and rich cultural practices. Among its many achievements, the use of gold stands out as a significant aspect of its socio-economic and cultural landscape, reflecting the civilization's intricate trade networks, artistic endeavors, and social hierarchies.

Economic Importance of Gold
Gold played a crucial role in the economy of the Indus Valley Civilization, serving as a medium of exchange and a store of value. The abundance of natural resources in the region facilitated trade with neighboring cultures, particularly with Mesopotamia, where gold was highly prized. Archaeological evidence suggests that the Indus Valley had access to gold from various sources, including local deposits and imports from regions such as the Iranian plateau. This access enabled the civilization to not only maintain its local economy but also integrate into wider trade networks, which relied heavily on precious metals as symbols of wealth and power.

The presence of gold artifacts, including jewelry, tools, and decorative items, indicates that gold was not merely a means of trade but also a status symbol among the elite. The sophistication of these artifacts, often intricately designed and adorned with semi-precious stones, speaks to the skilled craftsmanship prevalent in the Indus Valley. Goldsmiths and artisans played a pivotal role in the economy, producing items that reflected both the aesthetic values and the social hierarchies of their communities.

Cultural and Religious Significance
Gold had profound cultural and religious implications within the Indus Valley Civilization. While the lack of deciphered written records makes it challenging to ascertain the exact spiritual beliefs of the people, the abundance of gold artifacts suggests that it was likely associated with divinity, purity, and immortality. Many of the gold items discovered at archaeological sites, such as the famed "Dancing Girl" figurine from Mohenjo-Daro, highlight the aesthetic and possibly ritualistic importance of gold in their society.

Moreover, gold was often utilized in burial practices, reflecting its significance in life and afterlife beliefs. The discovery of gold ornaments in graves indicates that these items were not only markers of wealth but also symbols of status in the afterlife. This practice underscores the connection between material wealth and spiritual beliefs, with gold serving as a bridge between the earthly realm and the divine.

Social Stratification
The distribution of gold artifacts across different strata of society in the Indus Valley provides insights into the social organization of this ancient civilization. While gold was accessible to the elite, evidence suggests that it was also present among the middle and lower classes, albeit in lesser quantities. This stratification indicates that wealth was concentrated among a ruling class who utilized gold to establish and maintain their status.

Artifacts such as gold jewelry and ornamental objects reveal not only the artistic capabilities of the Indus Valley craftsmen but also the societal values that prioritized luxury and display. The existence of specialized artisans and trade networks for gold further suggests a complex society where craftsmanship and commerce were integral to social identity.

Conclusion

In the Indus Valley Civilization, gold transcended its material value to embody economic, cultural, and symbolic significance. It facilitated trade, reflected social hierarchies, and played a vital role in religious practices. The legacy of gold in this ancient civilization provides a window into the complexities of their society, highlighting how a single material can shape and define human experience across various dimensions of life. As archaeological explorations continue to uncover the depths of the Indus Valley's history, the role of gold remains a testament to the civilization's sophistication and its lasting impact on South Asia's cultural heritage.

Gold in Ancient China: From Currency to Art

Gold has played a pivotal role in the history and culture of ancient China, serving not only as a form of currency but also as a medium for artistic expression and a symbol of power and prestige. The historical significance of gold in China can be traced back thousands of years, with its use evolving alongside the development of Chinese civilization.

Economic Significance

In ancient China, gold was highly valued for its rarity, beauty, and permanence. The earliest known use of gold as currency dates back to the Zhou Dynasty (1046-256 BCE), where it began to complement the traditional barter system. During this period, gold and bronze were often cast into coins, which facilitated trade and commerce across vast regions. The introduction of gold as currency marked a significant advancement in the economic infrastructure of ancient China, as it allowed for standardized trade practices and the growth of a more complex economy.

By the time of the Han Dynasty (206 BCE-220 CE), gold coins were widely circulated, reflecting the wealth of the state and the prosperity of its citizens. Gold was not only used for everyday transactions but also as a reserve of value, providing stability during economic fluctuations. The significance of gold in trade extended beyond China's borders, influencing relationships with neighboring cultures along the Silk Road, where it functioned as a medium of exchange for silk, spices, and other precious goods.

Artistic Expression

Beyond its economic utility, gold was integral to the artistic heritage of ancient China. Goldsmiths produced intricate jewelry, ceremonial objects, and decorative art pieces that showcased the metal's luster and malleability. The craftsmanship involved in creating gold artifacts was a testament to the skill and artistry of Chinese artisans. These creations often featured motifs that were significant in Chinese culture, such as dragons, phoenixes, and auspicious symbols representing prosperity and good fortune.

One of the most notable uses of gold in art was in the creation of funerary objects, particularly during the Shang (1600-1046 BCE) and Zhou Dynasties. Gold was often used in burial items, including masks, ornaments, and vessels, reflecting the belief in an afterlife where such treasures would accompany the deceased. The practice of interring gold with the dead underscored its status as a symbol of power and wealth, reserved for the elite and nobility.

Cultural Significance
Gold also held profound cultural and spiritual significance in ancient Chinese society. It was associated with the sun, representing light and life, and was believed to possess protective properties. The color gold symbolized wealth, nobility, and immortality, making it a preferred choice in rituals and ceremonies. During significant events, such as weddings and festivals, gold was often incorporated into attire and decorations, enhancing the auspiciousness of the occasion.

The importance of gold in governance and royal symbolism cannot be overstated. Emperors often adorned themselves with gold regalia, using the metal to convey authority and divine right. Gold objects were not only markers of status but also played a role in political diplomacy, with gifts of gold being exchanged between rulers to solidify alliances or signify goodwill.

Conclusion
In summary, gold in ancient China transcended its role as mere currency; it was a multifaceted element of society that influenced economic practices, artistic endeavors, and cultural beliefs. Its enduring legacy is evident in the rich history of Chinese civilization, where gold remains a revered symbol of wealth, beauty, and power. The intricate balance between its practical uses and its representation of ideals reflects the complexity and depth of ancient Chinese culture, making gold a significant thread in the tapestry of human history.

The Spread of Gold Use Across the Ancient World
Gold, with its unique properties and intrinsic allure, played a pivotal role in the development of trade and culture across ancient civilizations. Its early use in various regions laid the groundwork for complex economic systems, cultural exchanges, and the formation of socio-political hierarchies. As societies evolved, so too did the significance of gold, steering the course of human history in profound ways.

Economic Influence and Trade Networks

The allure of gold fostered extensive trade networks, connecting disparate regions and facilitating cultural exchanges. The earliest known gold artifacts date back to around 4000 BCE in regions like the Balkans and Anatolia, where gold was initially used for decorative purposes and as a medium of exchange. As trade routes developed, particularly in the context of the Silk Road, gold became an essential commodity that transcended geographic boundaries. It served not merely as currency but as a symbol of wealth and power, influencing the economic dynamics of civilizations from Mesopotamia to China.

In Mesopotamia, gold was integral to the economy, with city-states like Ur and Babylon establishing trade relationships that expanded their reach. Merchants traded goods such as textiles, grains, and spices for gold, which was highly valued not only for its beauty but also for its malleability and durability. The use of gold as a standard in commerce allowed for a more sophisticated economic structure, laying the foundation for future monetary systems.

Cultural Significance and Artistic Expression

The spread of gold use was not limited to trade alone; it also permeated cultural and religious practices. In ancient Egypt, gold was associated with the divine, often used in the creation of tombs and artifacts for the afterlife. The famous burial mask of Tutankhamun is a prime example of how gold was employed in artistic expression, symbolizing eternal life and the pharaoh's divine status. This cultural association with gold extended to other civilizations, influencing art, mythology, and religious practices.

In the Indus Valley Civilization, gold jewelry and ornaments signified status and prosperity, reflecting social stratification. The craftsmanship involved in goldsmithing not only showcased artistic talent but also contributed to the cultural identity of various regions. Artistic styles evolved, incorporating gold into religious icons, personal adornments, and ceremonial objects, thus reinforcing its cultural significance.

Political Implications and Power Dynamics

Gold's role extended into the political realm as well, serving as a tool for power consolidation and diplomacy. Rulers across ancient civilizations utilized gold to fund military campaigns, build monumental architecture, and enhance their status. In ancient Persia, for instance, the Achaemenid Empire leveraged gold to showcase wealth, both in domestic governance and in establishing dominance over neighboring territories.

Furthermore, the quest for gold often led to conflict and conquest, shaping the geopolitical landscape of the ancient world. The desire for gold spurred exploration and colonization, as seen with the expansion of empires that sought to control gold-rich territories. This pursuit of wealth through gold not only influenced trade routes but also led to the establishment of cultural exchanges, as conquering forces often integrated local practices, beliefs, and artistic expressions into their own cultures.

Conclusion
The spread of gold use across the ancient world was a multifaceted phenomenon that influenced trade, culture, and politics. Its role as a medium of exchange and a symbol of wealth facilitated the development of complex economic systems and cultural identities. The allure of gold not only enriched societies but also shaped the narrative of human history, leaving an enduring legacy that continues to resonate in our understanding of wealth, power, and artistic expression today. As civilizations interacted, gold became a universal language of value, bridging cultural divides and fostering connections that would influence the trajectory of human development for millennia.

Chapter 3

Gold in the Classical World

Gold in Ancient Greece

Gold has held a prominent position in ancient Greek society, intertwining both the realms of mythology and the practical aspects of economy. In Greece, gold was not merely a commodity; it was imbued with cultural, religious, and symbolic significance. This duality is evident in the tales of gods, heroes, and the economic practices of the time.

In mythology, gold is frequently associated with divine power and immortality. The ancient Greeks revered gold as a gift from the gods. The story of King Midas exemplifies this notion. Midas, who wished for the ability to turn everything he touched into gold, ultimately found that his greed brought him great despair, illustrating the idea that wealth without wisdom can lead to ruin. This myth not only highlights gold's allure but also serves as a cautionary tale about the consequences of greed and the moral complexities surrounding wealth.

Furthermore, gold was often linked to the gods themselves. The ancient Greeks believed that the gods resided on Mount Olympus and were adorned with gold, representing their divine status. Temples dedicated to various deities were often decorated with gold, emphasizing its importance in religious practices. The Parthenon, dedicated to Athena, featured a massive gold and ivory statue of the goddess, symbolizing the wealth and power of Athens during its Golden Age. Such representations reinforced the idea of gold as a medium through which humans could connect with the divine.

Economically, gold played a crucial role in the trade and commerce of ancient Greece. As city-states bartered goods, gold became a standard of value, facilitating trade across regions. The adoption of gold coins, particularly during the reign of King Croesus of Lydia in the 6th century BCE, revolutionized the economy. These coins, stamped with images of rulers and deities, standardized currency and allowed for more efficient transactions. The use of gold coins helped to solidify trade relationships with neighboring regions and laid the groundwork for a more interconnected Mediterranean economy.

Gold also had practical applications beyond currency. The Greeks utilized gold in various crafts, including jewelry, armor, and decorative items. Artisans skillfully crafted exquisite pieces that showcased not only their skill but also the wealth of their patrons. This craftsmanship reflected the social hierarchy of the time; those who could afford gold adorned themselves with intricate designs, signaling their status and influence within society. The goldsmiths of ancient Greece were highly regarded, and their work contributed to the cultural legacy of the era.

However, the quest for gold was not without its darker aspects. The pursuit of gold led to conflicts and conquests, as city-states vied for control of resources and territory. The desire for wealth often instigated wars, such as the conflicts between Athens and Sparta. These struggles illustrated the lengths to which societies would go to amass wealth and the inherent tensions that gold could exacerbate.

In conclusion, gold in ancient Greece served as a multifaceted symbol of wealth, divinity, and societal power. Its presence in mythology reflected the cultural values of the time, while its role in the economy facilitated trade and commerce. The artisanship associated with gold, along with its implications for social status, further entrenched its significance within Greek culture. Gold's dual existence as a mythical object and a practical resource underscores its lasting legacy in shaping ancient Greek society and its influence on subsequent civilizations. As such, the story of gold in ancient Greece remains a testament to the complex relationship between humanity and this precious metal.

Gold in the Roman Empire: Wealth and Power

The Roman Empire, one of the most influential civilizations in history, had a profound relationship with gold that underscored its economic strength and social hierarchy. Gold, considered the epitome of wealth, was central to Rome's monetary system, its economy, and its cultural identity.

Economic Significance of Gold

The Romans utilized gold extensively as a medium of exchange and a store of value. The introduction of gold coins, particularly the aureus, marked a significant evolution in Roman currency. The aureus was made from high-purity gold and weighed about 8 grams, becoming a standard for trade across the vast territories of the Empire. This coinage facilitated commerce, allowing for more complex economic transactions and solidifying gold's status as a reliable currency. The stability of the gold standard helped maintain economic order, especially in times of political upheaval and war.

Gold was also vital for the treasury of the Roman Empire. The accumulation of gold was seen as a reflection of the empire's power and prosperity. Emperors would often showcase their wealth through vast reserves of gold, which were used to pay for military campaigns, public works, and lavish games and festivals. The imperial treasury, known as the fiscus, was heavily stocked with gold, ensuring the state could respond to economic challenges and military needs.

Social Hierarchy and Display of Wealth

In Roman society, gold signified not just wealth but also status and power. The elite class adorned themselves with gold jewelry and luxurious items, which served as a visual representation of their wealth. Gold became synonymous with prestige, and the more gold one possessed, the higher one's social standing. Senators and wealthy citizens would often flaunt their wealth in public, wearing intricate gold rings and necklaces that showcased their affluence.

Gold was also used in art and architecture to celebrate the grandeur of the empire. Gold leaf and gilding adorned temples, public buildings, and monuments, illustrating the Romans' reverence for wealth. The Colosseum, for example, featured gold-plated decorations, exemplifying how gold was integral not only to personal wealth but also to the identity of the empire itself.

Gold in Warfare and Conquest

The Romans recognized the strategic importance of gold in warfare. Military campaigns were often motivated by the desire to acquire gold from conquered territories. The spoils of war included not only gold coins but also gold artifacts, jewelry, and other valuable objects. The acquisition of gold through conquest was a symbol of Roman superiority and military prowess. The famous phrase "Vae Victis!" or "Woe to the vanquished!" encapsulates the Romans' ruthless pursuit of wealth through military dominance.

Additionally, the Roman army was paid in gold, which incentivized soldiers and ensured loyalty. The promise of gold rewards for valor in battle motivated troops, contributing to the empire's military success and expansion. This reliance on gold for military funding further solidified its importance in the Roman economic and political landscape.

Cultural and Religious Dimensions

Gold also held significant cultural and religious connotations in Roman society. It was used in rituals and offerings to the gods, reinforcing the connection between wealth and divine favor. Temples were often adorned with gold, and the act of donating gold to temples was seen as a way to gain social prestige and divine blessings.

In conclusion, gold in the Roman Empire was not merely a commodity but a central pillar of its economy, a symbol of social hierarchy, and a tool for military conquest. Its multifaceted role contributed to the empire's enduring legacy of wealth and power, illustrating how gold shaped the political, social, and cultural fabric of one of history's greatest civilizations. As a result, the influence of gold in Rome laid the groundwork for its continued significance in later societies and economies.

Gold in Ancient Persia: Kings and Conquests

The Achaemenid Empire, which flourished from the 6th to the 4th centuries BCE, is renowned for its vast territorial expanse, sophisticated administrative systems, and remarkable architectural achievements. However, one of the most notable aspects of this empire was its profound relationship with gold, which served not only as a symbol of wealth and power but also as a crucial component in the functioning of its economy and military.

Gold in Ancient Persia was integral to the Achaemenid rulers' strategies for consolidating power and displaying their authority. The Persian kings, such as Cyrus the Great, Darius I, and Xerxes I, utilized gold extensively to forge an image of divinity and legitimacy. Gold was viewed as a manifestation of the divine right to rule; as a result, it was often used in the creation of opulent thrones, palatial decorations, and ceremonial regalia. The grandeur of these items was designed to impress subjects and foreign dignitaries alike, reinforcing the notion that the Persian kings were chosen by the gods to lead.

The significance of gold extended beyond its aesthetic appeal; it was a driving force in the economic structure of the Achaemenid Empire. Gold coins, known as "darics," were introduced by Darius I as a means to standardize currency across the empire, facilitating trade and commerce. This standardization not only simplified transactions but also promoted economic stability and growth. The daric, minted in gold, became a widely accepted form of currency that allowed for the flourishing of trade networks across the Mediterranean and into the East, contributing to the empire's immense wealth.

Gold also played a crucial role in the military endeavors of the Achaemenids. The empire was marked by a series of military conquests that expanded its borders significantly. To finance these campaigns, the Persian kings relied on their gold reserves, using the wealth amassed from taxes and tributes collected from subjugated nations. The ability to fund large-scale military operations was essential for maintaining control over such a vast territory, and the abundance of gold allowed for the recruitment of mercenaries and the procurement of advanced weaponry.

In addition to its role in the military and economy, gold held significant cultural and religious weight in the Achaemenid Empire. The Persians believed that gold had sacred qualities, often associating it with the divine. Temples and religious artifacts adorned with gold reflected the empire's spiritual values and were integral to rituals and ceremonies. The use of gold in religious contexts helped to solidify the connection between the monarchy and the divine, further legitimizing the authority of the Persian kings.

Moreover, the artistry associated with Persian goldsmiths during this period was remarkable. Artisans crafted exquisite jewelry, ceremonial vessels, and decorative items that showcased intricate designs and techniques. These items not only served as symbols of wealth but also demonstrated the artistic and cultural sophistication of the Achaemenid Empire.

In summary, gold in Ancient Persia was a multifaceted resource that transcended mere material wealth. It was a tool of political power, a cornerstone of economic stability, a means of military financing, and a symbol of divine favor. The Achaemenid Empire's ability to harness the significance of gold contributed to its status as one of the most powerful and influential civilizations of the ancient world, leaving a lasting legacy in the annals of history.

Gold and the Silk Road: Trade Across Continents

The Silk Road, an ancient network of trade routes connecting the East and the West, played a pivotal role in the cultural, economic, and political exchanges that shaped civilizations from China to the Mediterranean. Spanning over 4,000 miles, this expansive route facilitated not only the exchange of goods like silk, spices, and precious metals but also ideas, art, and technologies. Among the most significant commodities traded along this route was gold, which served as a symbol of wealth and a medium of exchange that transcended borders and cultures.

Gold's allure is timeless, making it a staple of trade for millennia. In the context of the Silk Road, gold represented more than mere monetary value; it was also a symbol of power, prestige, and divine favor. The demand for gold in various regions drove merchants to seek new sources, prompting extensive trade networks that included not just gold itself but also gold-adorned artifacts, jewelry, and currency.

The East, particularly in regions like China, had a long-standing tradition of valuing gold for its beauty and rarity. During the Han Dynasty (206 BCE – 220 CE), gold was used in coinage, and the imperial courts were adorned with gold ornaments, showcasing the metal's significance in both economic and cultural terms. The Chinese also used gold as a means of tribute, sending gold to neighboring states as a display of power and influence. As trade flourished along the Silk Road, this demand for gold created a reciprocal relationship. As Chinese silk gained popularity in the West, it was often traded for gold, which was then used by artisans to create exquisite crafts and luxury items.

Conversely, regions in the West, such as the Roman Empire, were eager to acquire the luxurious goods and fine silk produced in the East. Gold served as a key currency to facilitate these transactions. Roman coins, often minted from gold, were widely accepted across the Silk Road, allowing merchants to engage in trade with relative ease. The Romans valued gold not only for its intrinsic worth but also for its role in demonstrating wealth and power. The influx of silk and spices into Rome, accompanied by a robust flow of gold, significantly impacted the economy and culture of the empire.

The Persian Empire also played a crucial role in this trade network. Control of vital trade routes allowed Persian merchants to facilitate the flow of gold between the East and West. Persian coins, often made of gold, became a standard medium for trade, ensuring that transactions could occur seamlessly across diverse cultures. The Achaemenid Empire's strategic positioning along the Silk Road allowed it to capitalize on the lucrative trade of gold, serving as both a facilitator and beneficiary of this exchange.

Beyond the immediate economic implications, the trade of gold along the Silk Road also fostered cultural exchanges that enriched societies on both ends. The movement of gold artifacts, for instance, introduced new artistic styles and techniques, influencing everything from pottery to architecture. This cross-cultural interaction led to a shared appreciation for craftsmanship and aesthetics, further deepening the ties between distant civilizations.

Moreover, the quest for gold spurred exploration and the establishment of new trade routes. Merchants and travelers, driven by the promise of wealth, ventured into uncharted territories, often facing perilous conditions. These journeys not only expanded the geographic reach of trade but also facilitated the exchange of knowledge, technology, and cultural practices.

In conclusion, gold was not merely a commodity traded along the Silk Road; it was a powerful catalyst that facilitated economic interaction, cultural exchange, and the establishment of complex networks that linked diverse civilizations. The legacy of this precious metal continues to resonate today, reminding us of the profound impact that trade and commerce have on human history. The Silk Road exemplifies how gold, in its various forms, played a crucial role in shaping the interconnected world we inhabit.

Gold as a Symbol of Divinity and Power

Throughout history, gold has transcended its material value to become a potent symbol of divinity and authority in many ancient cultures. Its intrinsic properties—luster, durability, and rarity—have made it a fitting representation of the celestial, the eternal, and the divine. This section explores how gold functioned not only as a medium of exchange but also as a manifestation of power, often intertwined with religious beliefs and royal authority.

In ancient Egypt, gold was closely associated with the gods and the afterlife. The Egyptians believed that gold was the flesh of the sun god Ra, which imbued it with divine significance. This belief was vividly illustrated in the burial practices of pharaohs, where gold artifacts, including masks, jewelry, and sarcophagi, were interred with the dead. The most famous example is the golden mask of Tutankhamun, which served to protect the pharaoh in the afterlife and solidify his status as a deity among mortals. The use of gold in funerary rites underscored the belief in the pharaoh's divine right to rule, as it was thought that the wealth and opulence of their burial would ensure their favor in the afterlife.

Similarly, in Mesopotamia, gold represented both wealth and divine favor. The Sumerians and Babylonians crafted intricate gold jewelry and religious artifacts, often dedicated to their deities. Gold was used to adorn temples and statues, reinforcing the notion that the divine was both precious and powerful. The famous Ishtar Gate, adorned with gold and lapis lazuli, exemplifies how gold was not merely decorative but also a physical manifestation of the power of the gods.

The symbolic association of gold with divinity extended to the Indus Valley Civilization, where gold objects have been unearthed at sites like Mohenjo-Daro. These artifacts suggest that gold was used in rituals and as offerings to deities, highlighting its role in spiritual practices. The absence of extensive written records from this civilization leaves much to speculation, but the presence of gold in religious contexts indicates its importance as a symbol of the divine.

In ancient China, gold held a dual significance as both a material wealth and a symbol of imperial authority. The ruling dynasties used gold to reinforce their power and legitimacy. The emperors adorned themselves with gold jewelry, and the use of gold in ceremonial objects emphasized their divine right to rule. In Confucianism and Taoism, gold was often associated with prosperity and harmony, further embedding it into the cultural fabric as a symbol of order and stability.

Gold's role as a symbol of power was not limited to ancient civilizations; it also permeated the cultures of the classical world. In Greece and Rome, gold coins became a standard for wealth and influenced political power dynamics. The imagery on these coins often depicted gods and goddesses, reinforcing the idea that those who possessed gold were favored by the divine. Roman emperors, in particular, utilized gold to project their power and authority, minting coins that bore their likeness alongside divine symbols.

Overall, gold has served as a multifaceted symbol of divinity and power across various ancient cultures. Its enduring allure and intrinsic qualities have made it a pervasive motif in human history, where it frequently represented the intersection of the material and the sacred. This deep-rooted association has left an indelible mark on how societies perceive authority, wealth, and the divine, maintaining gold's status as a timeless emblem of human aspiration and reverence.

Chapter 4

The Middle Ages

The Role of Gold in Medieval Europe

The medieval period, spanning from the 5th to the late 15th century, was a transformative era in European history characterized by feudalism, the rise of monarchies, and shifting economic structures. Central to this transformation was gold, which played a pivotal role in shaping both the economy and the political landscape of Europe.

Economic Influence

Gold served as a fundamental pillar of medieval economies, acting as a medium of exchange, a store of value, and a unit of account. Initially, barter systems dominated trade, but as commerce expanded, the need for a standardized currency became apparent. Gold coins emerged as the preferred currency, with notable examples such as the Byzantine solidus, the Carolingian denier, and the Venetian ducat. These coins not only facilitated trade within regions but also across borders, enabling merchants to engage in long-distance trade routes, including the Silk Road.

Gold's scarcity and durability made it an ideal choice for currency, reinforcing its status as a symbol of wealth. As trade networks grew, so did the demand for gold. This led to the establishment of various trading hubs and marketplaces, where gold coins circulated freely. The rise of banking institutions in cities like Florence and Venice further solidified gold's economic significance. These banks began to accept deposits and issue promissory notes, which could be exchanged for gold, thereby increasing liquidity in the economy and facilitating commerce.

Political Ramifications

The political implications of gold in medieval Europe were profound. Monarchs and nobles sought to amass gold not only for personal wealth but also to fund their ambitions, whether military campaigns, territorial expansion, or lavish court life. The accumulation of gold became synonymous with power, as rulers who possessed it could maintain armies, build fortifications, and engage in diplomacy with wealthier nations.

The interplay between gold and politics is exemplified by the practice of coinage. Kings often issued their own currency, which not only represented their sovereignty but also served as a means to display their wealth and authority. This practice became particularly pronounced during the reign of Charlemagne, who standardized coinage across his empire to enhance trade and economic stability while reinforcing his political power.

Moreover, the quest for gold catalyzed numerous conflicts and power struggles. The Crusades, for instance, were driven not only by religious fervor but also by the desire to control lucrative trade routes and access gold reserves in the East. The wealth acquired through these campaigns often funded further military endeavors, creating a vicious cycle of war and wealth accumulation.

Cultural Significance
Gold also permeated the cultural fabric of medieval society. It adorned religious artifacts, books, and architecture, symbolizing divine favor and connection to the sacred. The opulence of gold in cathedrals and monasteries reflected both the wealth of the Church and its powerful influence in society. This intertwining of gold with religious and political authority contributed to the perception of gold as a divine gift, further entrenching its status in the societal hierarchy.

As the medieval era progressed, the discovery of new gold reserves in the Americas during the Age of Exploration would eventually shift the center of gold's influence. However, throughout the Middle Ages, gold remained a crucial element in shaping the economy, politics, and culture of Europe. Its enduring legacy is evident in the development of modern financial systems and the continued association of gold with wealth and power. Thus, the role of gold in medieval Europe was not merely that of a valuable commodity; it was a catalyst for change, shaping the course of history and the dynamics of human society.

Gold in the Byzantine Empire: Continuity and Change

The Byzantine Empire, which emerged from the eastern half of the Roman Empire after its division in the late 4th century AD, was a remarkable civilization that maintained and transformed the traditions of gold usage established in antiquity. Gold in the Byzantine Empire symbolized power, wealth, and divine favor, serving both as a medium of exchange and a material for artistic expression. The Byzantine approach to gold was characterized by continuity in tradition, yet marked by significant changes that reflected the empire's evolving political, economic, and cultural landscapes.

Continuity of Gold Traditions
Byzantium inherited a rich legacy of gold craftsmanship from the Roman Empire, which had established gold not only as a currency but also as a status symbol. The solidus, a gold coin introduced by Emperor Constantine I in the early 4th century, became a standard currency throughout the empire and was widely accepted in international trade. The solidus not only

facilitated commerce but also served as a reflection of the economic stability and strength of the Byzantine state. Its long-lasting influence can be seen in the designs that adorned the coins, often featuring the emperor's image and Christian symbols, thereby merging political power with religious authority.

Artisans in the Byzantine Empire continued the tradition of exquisite goldsmithing, creating intricate jewelry, religious artifacts, and liturgical items. Churches and monasteries were adorned with gold-plated icons, chalices, and vestments, which served both aesthetic and spiritual purposes. The use of gold in these contexts not only reinforced the wealth of the church but also emphasized the divine right of the Byzantine emperors, who were often seen as Christ's representatives on earth.

Transformation in Gold Usage
While the Byzantine Empire maintained many Roman traditions, it also adapted and transformed its gold practices in response to changing circumstances. The rise of Christianity as the state religion significantly altered the symbolism attached to gold. In contrast to the Roman focus on imperial power and military conquest, Byzantine gold increasingly represented divine authority and spiritual wealth. This shift is evident in the use of gold in religious iconography, where the material was employed to create images of saints and Christ that elevated the sacred above the secular.

Economically, the Byzantine Empire faced various challenges, including invasions, trade disruptions, and internal strife. These pressures led to innovations in gold usage, particularly in the realm of finance. The empire developed sophisticated banking practices, where gold was used not only in coinage but also in deposits and loans. The establishment of state-controlled mints ensured the regulation of gold currency, reflecting a shift towards a more centralized economic system. This transformation allowed Byzantium to maintain its economic stability amidst fluctuating external conditions.

Moreover, Byzantine trade networks expanded significantly, connecting the empire to Asia and Europe. Gold became a crucial commodity in these interactions, with Byzantine merchants importing and exporting gold artifacts and coins that influenced the economies of neighboring regions. The impact of this trade was profound, as it allowed for cultural exchanges and the dissemination of Byzantine artistic styles, particularly in goldwork.

Conclusion
In summary, the Byzantine Empire's relationship with gold exemplified a fascinating blend of continuity and change. While it preserved the rich traditions of gold usage from the Roman era,

it also adapted these practices to reflect its unique religious, economic, and cultural context. Gold remained a vital element of Byzantine identity, symbolizing divine authority and economic stability. Through its exquisite craftsmanship and innovative economic practices, the Byzantine Empire not only maintained its golden legacy but also ensured that gold continued to be a potent symbol of power and spirituality in a rapidly changing world.

The Islamic Golden Age: Gold in Science and Trade

The Islamic Golden Age, spanning from the 8th to the 14th century, marked an extraordinary period of cultural, scientific, and economic flourishing in the Islamic world. During this era, gold played a pivotal role not only as a symbol of wealth but also as a catalyst for scientific advancement and trade. The Islamic civilizations, which included a vast expanse from Spain to India, became centers of knowledge and commerce, greatly influencing the global economy and the development of various scientific fields.

The Economic Significance of Gold

Gold's intrinsic value made it a critical component of trade and commerce in the Islamic world. The establishment of a robust economy was facilitated by the use of gold coins, particularly the dinar, which became a standard currency across vast territories. This encouraged trade not only within the Islamic empire but also with neighboring regions, including Europe, Africa, and Asia. The flourishing trade networks, exemplified by the Silk Road and maritime routes, were vital for the exchange of goods, ideas, and innovations. Merchants utilized gold not only for transactions but also as a medium for building trust and establishing credit, which was essential for long-distance trade.

Advancements in Science and Technology

During the Islamic Golden Age, scholars made remarkable contributions to various scientific disciplines, many of which were supported by the wealth derived from gold and trade. The wealth generated from gold mining and commerce allowed for the patronage of scholars, resulting in the establishment of centers of learning, such as the House of Wisdom in Baghdad. This institution became a hub for intellectual exchange, where scholars translated ancient texts and conducted original research.

One of the most notable advancements was in the field of chemistry, which was heavily influenced by alchemy. Alchemists, such as Jabir ibn Hayyan, sought to understand the properties and transformations of substances, including gold. They developed techniques for distillation, crystallization, and the creation of acids, which laid the groundwork for modern chemistry. The quest to transmute base metals into gold, while largely symbolic, spurred significant experimental practices that advanced scientific understanding.

Gold in Art and Architecture
Gold was not only a medium of exchange but also a critical element in art and architecture during the Islamic Golden Age. Islamic artisans excelled in the use of gold leaf and goldsmithing, resulting in exquisite pieces of jewelry, decorative art, and architectural embellishments. Mosques and palaces were adorned with gold, signifying wealth and divine splendor. The intricate designs often reflected a blend of cultural influences, showcasing the interconnectedness of the Islamic world with other civilizations.

The Role of Gold in Cultural Exchange
The trade networks established during the Islamic Golden Age facilitated the exchange of not just goods but also ideas, technologies, and cultural practices. Gold acted as a currency that transcended linguistic and cultural barriers, promoting interactions among diverse populations. This exchange enriched Islamic scholarship and culture, allowing for the assimilation of knowledge from ancient Greece, Persia, India, and beyond. The resulting syncretism fostered a vibrant intellectual climate that propelled advancements in mathematics, astronomy, medicine, and philosophy.

Conclusion
In summary, the Islamic Golden Age was a transformative period in which gold played a central role in science and trade. The wealth generated through gold facilitated economic prosperity, intellectual advancements, and cultural exchanges that significantly influenced the trajectory of human civilization. The legacy of this era continues to resonate today, illustrating the profound impact of gold as a driver of both economic and intellectual progress. The interplay between gold, commerce, and knowledge during this period exemplifies how material wealth can foster a flourishing society, making the Islamic Golden Age a pivotal chapter in the history of gold.

The African Gold Kingdoms: Mali and Ghana
The African kingdoms of Mali and Ghana stand as monumental examples of the historical significance of gold in Africa. Situated in West Africa, these kingdoms not only exemplified wealth through their abundant gold resources but also displayed the profound influence that gold had on trade, culture, and international relations during their respective eras.

The Kingdom of Ghana (circa 300-1200 AD)
Often referred to as the "Land of Gold," the Kingdom of Ghana was one of the earliest and most prosperous empires in West Africa. The kingdom's wealth stemmed from its strategic control over the trans-Saharan trade routes that connected the gold-rich regions of West Africa with the Mediterranean economies. Ghana was not a gold-producing region per se; rather, it served as a commercial hub where gold was traded for salt, textiles, and other commodities. The kings of

Ghana imposed taxes on the gold and goods that passed through their territory, thereby accumulating vast wealth and solidifying their power.

The economy of Ghana thrived on the lucrative trade of gold, which was in high demand across North Africa and beyond. The famous traveler and historian, Ibn Battuta, noted that the wealth of the Ghanaian king was so immense that he was said to possess a gold throne and could command respect and loyalty from his subjects. The use of gold in this context transcended mere currency; it was a symbol of royalty and divine favor.

The Mali Empire (circa 1235-1600 AD)

Following the decline of Ghana, the Mali Empire emerged as a dominant force in West Africa, largely due to its control over gold production and trade. Under the rule of Mansa Musa, who reigned from 1312 to 1337, Mali reached its zenith, becoming one of the richest empires in history. Mansa Musa is famously known for his pilgrimage to Mecca in 1324, during which he reportedly distributed gold so generously that he caused a temporary devaluation of the metal in regions he passed through.

Mali's wealth was not solely based on gold; it also embraced agriculture, education, and culture. The city of Timbuktu became a center for Islamic scholarship and trade, attracting scholars and traders from distant lands. The Mali Empire's commitment to education and culture fostered an environment where the arts flourished alongside economic prosperity. The university of Sankore in Timbuktu became a beacon of knowledge, drawing students from various parts of Africa and the Middle East.

Trade Networks and Influence

Both Ghana and Mali were pivotal in shaping the trans-Saharan trade networks. Their gold was sought after by traders from North Africa and Europe, who exchanged goods such as salt, textiles, and luxury items. This trade not only enriched the kingdoms but also facilitated cultural exchanges and the spread of Islam, which became a significant aspect of governance and daily life in these empires.

The influence of these kingdoms extended beyond their immediate geographical boundaries. The wealth generated from gold allowed Mali and Ghana to engage in diplomacy and establish alliances with neighboring states and distant powers, showcasing gold's role as a medium of exchange not only in commerce but also in politics.

In conclusion, the African gold kingdoms of Mali and Ghana were more than just wealthy empires; they were foundational to the development of trade, culture, and political structures in

West Africa. Their legacies of wealth, power, and influence continue to resonate today, reminding us of the central role that gold played in shaping human history and societal development in the region. These kingdoms serve as a testament to how natural resources, when strategically managed, can elevate civilizations and foster complex networks of interaction that extend well beyond their borders.

Gold and the Crusades: Financing War and Religion

The Crusades, a series of religious wars initiated by European Christians between the late 11th and late 13th centuries, were driven by a complex interplay of faith, territorial ambition, and socio-political dynamics. Central to the success of these military campaigns was the role of gold—not merely as a currency but as a critical resource that funded the ambitions of kings, knights, and the Church itself. The quest for gold was intertwined with the broader objectives of the Crusades, as it provided the financial means to support extensive military expeditions, establish fortified settlements, and maintain the logistics necessary for prolonged campaigns in the Holy Land.

Financial Foundations of the Crusades

The First Crusade (1096-1099) was largely funded by a combination of royal treasury resources, donations from the nobility, and contributions from the Church. The Pope played a vital role in galvanizing financial support through the promise of spiritual rewards, including indulgences and the forgiveness of sins for those who participated. Wealthy patrons were encouraged to invest in the Crusades, often in the form of loans or donations. As the campaigns progressed, the need for sustained funding became apparent, leading to the establishment of financial structures that would facilitate this need.

The Role of Gold in Logistics and Supply

Gold was crucial in securing the necessary supplies and resources for the Crusaders on their journey to the Holy Land. In an era where coinage was the primary means of transaction, gold coins held significant value and were used to purchase provisions, weapons, and armor. Additionally, gold enabled the Crusaders to forge crucial alliances with local powers and to bribe hostile factions, ensuring smoother passage through foreign territories. The ability to wield wealth, particularly gold, often determined the Crusaders' success or failure in securing vital resources and support.

Economic Impact and Trade

The Crusades profoundly influenced trade routes and economic interactions between Europe and the East. The demand for gold increased as Crusaders returned with precious metals acquired from their conquests. The influx of gold into Europe contributed to the rise of merchant classes who facilitated trade, leading to the establishment of new trade routes and markets. The capture of Jerusalem and other key cities resulted in significant wealth accumulation, which was then reinvested in further military campaigns and the establishment of Crusader states. This cycle of wealth generation and expenditure created a burgeoning economy influenced by the desire for gold.

The Church and Gold

The Church's involvement in the Crusades was not solely spiritual; it was also financial. The Church's coffers were filled with gold from donations made by those seeking spiritual merit through participation in the Crusades. The promise of land, titles, and wealth in the conquered territories attracted many nobles, whose motivations were often as much about acquiring gold and resources as they were about religious fervor. Furthermore, the Church utilized gold to fund the construction of cathedrals and religious institutions, which would serve as symbols of faith and power in the newly established Crusader states.

The Consequences of Gold-Driven Campaigns

While the pursuit of gold facilitated the Crusades, it also led to severe consequences for both the Crusaders and the native populations of the conquered territories. The insatiable quest for wealth resulted in violence, exploitation, and the destabilization of local economies. Indigenous populations were often subjected to harsh treatment as Crusaders sought to extract resources, including gold. The legacy of these gold-driven campaigns is complex, as they contributed to both the flourishing of medieval European economies and the suffering of countless individuals in the regions impacted by the Crusades.

Conclusion

In summary, gold was more than just a means of exchange; it was the lifeblood of the Crusades, fueling the ambitions and conflicts that characterized this tumultuous period. The intertwined nature of war and wealth during the Crusades illustrates how gold has historically acted as a powerful motivator for human action, shaping the course of history in profound ways. The financial imperatives of the Crusades not only transformed the landscape of medieval Europe but also established enduring patterns of trade, power dynamics, and socio-political relationships that resonate to this day.

Chapter 5

The Age of Exploration and Gold

The Gold of the New World

The allure of gold has long been a potent motivator in human history, but few episodes illustrate its power as vividly as the era of European exploration and colonization of the New World. The quest for gold during the late 15th and early 16th centuries not only drove individual adventurers to seek fame and fortune but also catalyzed significant geopolitical transformations, reshaping the Americas and Europe alike.

The Age of Exploration, which began in earnest after Christopher Columbus's voyages in 1492, was fueled by tales of vast wealth and resources awaiting discovery in the Americas. The Spanish crown, in particular, was eager to expand its empire and increase its coffers. The initial expeditions were motivated by Renaissance ideals of glory, discovery, and the desire for new trade routes, but the discovery of gold quickly overshadowed these ambitions.

Explorers like Hernán Cortés and Francisco Pizarro became emblematic of this gold rush. Cortés's expedition to Mexico in 1519 led to the downfall of the Aztec Empire, driven largely by the pursuit of gold. The Spaniards, armed with superior weaponry and the devastating impact of diseases like smallpox, overwhelmed the indigenous populations. Cortés was drawn to the fabled wealth of the Aztecs, which was said to be concentrated in their capital city, Tenochtitlán. Upon encountering the vast reserves of gold and silver, Cortés's ambitions transformed from mere exploration to conquest and colonization. The riches he plundered enabled Spain to finance further conquests and solidify its dominance in the New World.

Similarly, Pizarro's conquest of the Inca Empire in the 1530s was motivated by reports of unimaginable wealth hidden in the Andes. With fewer than 200 men, Pizarro captured the Inca emperor Atahualpa and demanded a room filled with gold as ransom. Once the gold was collected, Pizarro executed Atahualpa, plunging the Inca civilization into chaos and enabling Spanish control over vast territories. The gold extracted from these regions flowed back to Spain, significantly altering its economy and allowing it to establish itself as a dominant power in Europe.

The quest for gold extended beyond mere extraction; it influenced trade patterns and prompted the establishment of a transatlantic trade network. The wealth derived from gold and silver mining in the Americas facilitated trade with Europe and Asia, leading to the rise of mercantilism. European nations sought to control trade routes and resources, leading to fierce competition and conflicts among colonial powers.

However, the relentless pursuit of gold had devastating consequences for indigenous populations. The demographic collapse due to disease, enslavement, and violent conquest resulted in the profound disruption of native cultures and societies. The encomienda system, where Spanish colonizers were granted rights to forced labor from indigenous people, exemplified the exploitation driven by the insatiable demand for precious metals.

Moreover, the quest for gold extended beyond the Spanish Empire. Other European powers, including the French, Portuguese, and later the British, were drawn into the Americas by similar promises of wealth. This competition for resources fueled colonization efforts, leading to the establishment of settlements and the growth of colonial economies based on the extraction of resources, including gold.

In summary, the quest for gold during the era of exploration not only spurred significant advancements in navigation and cartography but also facilitated the establishment of European empires at the expense of indigenous cultures. The gold of the New World was more than just a symbol of wealth; it was a catalyst for profound change, shaping the course of history for both the Old World and the New. The legacies of these actions continue to resonate today, influencing global economics, politics, and discussions surrounding colonialism and its lasting impacts on indigenous populations.

The Gold Rushes: California, Australia, and Beyond

The gold rushes of the 19th century were pivotal events that not only transformed the landscapes of the places they occurred but also had profound economic, social, and cultural implications that shaped the modern world. The most famous of these, the California Gold Rush, commenced in 1848, but similar booms occurred in Australia, Canada, and South Africa, each contributing uniquely to the global narrative of gold.

The California Gold Rush

The California Gold Rush began in January 1848 when James W. Marshall discovered gold at Sutter's Mill in Coloma, California. News of the discovery spread rapidly, and by 1849, an estimated 300,000 people had flocked to California, drawn by the promise of instant wealth. This influx of fortune seekers, known as "49ers," transformed California's demographics and economy. The state's population exploded, leading to the establishment of new towns, the expansion of infrastructure, and a significant boost to the economy.

The rush also had adverse effects, particularly on indigenous populations. The influx of settlers led to land dispossession, violence, and the decimation of native cultures. Moreover, the environmental impact was substantial, as rivers were diverted, forests cleared, and landscapes altered in the quest for gold.

The Australian Gold Rush

Around the same time, Australia experienced its own series of gold rushes beginning in the early 1850s, with significant discoveries in New South Wales and Victoria. The Australian Gold Rush attracted both local settlers and immigrants from around the world, including Chinese, British, and Irish. By 1852, more than 370,000 people had migrated to Australia, leading to a population boom and significant cultural diversification.

The gold rushes in Australia not only stimulated the economy, leading to the establishment of banks and businesses, but also underscored the country's colonial dynamics. The influx of Chinese miners led to cultural exchanges but also to racial tensions and policies aimed at restricting their participation. These events shaped Australian society and informed debates about immigration and national identity that persist to this day.

Beyond California and Australia

Other regions also experienced significant gold rushes that contributed to their historical trajectories. The Fraser River Gold Rush in British Columbia in 1858 attracted thousands to Canada, influencing the region's development and leading to the establishment of British Columbia as a province. Similarly, the discovery of gold in South Africa in the late 19th century, particularly in the Witwatersrand area, led to the Second Boer War and had lasting effects on the region's geopolitics and economy.

Economic and Social Impact

The gold rushes catalyzed major economic shifts, transitioning economies from agrarian to more diversified and industrialized systems. They spurred advancements in transportation, most notably railroads, which became crucial for moving people and goods. Cities like San Francisco emerged as bustling urban centers, while mining towns in Australia evolved into significant hubs of commerce and trade.

Socially, the gold rushes fostered a spirit of individualism and entrepreneurship. They created a culture of risk-taking and opportunity-seeking that defined much of the American and

Australian experience. However, they also highlighted issues of inequality and exploitation, particularly regarding labor practices, including the use of indentured labor and the marginalization of indigenous populations.

Conclusion

The gold rushes of California, Australia, and beyond were transformative events that reshaped societies and economies across continents. They not only contributed to the wealth of nations but also left legacies of conflict, environmental degradation, and cultural exchange. As major catalysts for change, these rushes played a crucial role in the evolution of modern economies and the social fabric of many countries, underscoring the enduring allure of gold as a symbol of opportunity and aspiration.

The Impact of Gold on Indigenous Populations

Gold has long been revered as a symbol of wealth and power, driving exploration and exploitation across the globe. However, the quest for gold has had profound and often devastating consequences for indigenous populations. The historical narrative of gold exploration is intertwined with colonization, land dispossession, cultural disruption, and socio-economic upheaval for many native communities.

The first significant impact of gold exploration on indigenous populations was the dramatic alteration of their landscapes and environments. As European powers and later American settlers sought gold, they often prioritized mining operations over the rights and lives of indigenous peoples. Large-scale mining operations decimated ecosystems, leading to soil erosion, deforestation, and the contamination of water sources. The environmental degradation caused by mining not only disrupted the delicate balance of local ecosystems but also undermined the traditional livelihoods of indigenous communities who depended on these natural resources for sustenance and cultural practices.

Moreover, the discovery of gold often led to the forced displacement of indigenous peoples from their ancestral lands. The California Gold Rush of the mid-19th century serves as a poignant example. Thousands of prospectors flooded into California, leading to violent conflicts with Native American tribes. The influx of settlers and miners resulted in the appropriation of land, the destruction of sacred sites, and the erosion of traditional ways of life. Similar patterns occurred in regions such as Australia, where the discovery of gold led to the dispossession of Aboriginal lands and their marginalization within their own territories.

In addition to physical displacement, gold exploration also had significant socio-economic impacts on indigenous populations. The introduction of a market economy, driven by gold mining, often disrupted traditional economies based on subsistence and communal sharing. Indigenous peoples were frequently coerced into participating in labor-intensive mining activities, which undermined their cultural practices and social structures. Many were subjected to exploitative labor conditions, receiving minimal compensation for their work, further entrenching cycles of poverty and dependency on the very systems that oppressed them.

Culturally, the pursuit of gold and the resulting colonization efforts led to the erosion of indigenous identities. Many communities faced the imposition of foreign values and belief systems that prioritized material wealth over communal well-being and spiritual connections to the land. Traditional knowledge and practices were often dismissed or actively suppressed, resulting in a loss of cultural heritage that resonates into the present day. The disruption of social structures and communal ties has had long-lasting effects, contributing to intergenerational trauma and challenges in maintaining cultural continuity.

Furthermore, the impact of gold exploration on indigenous populations extends into contemporary discussions surrounding land rights and reparations. Many indigenous groups continue to advocate for recognition of their rights to land and resources, often in opposition to mining companies and governmental policies that prioritize extraction over indigenous sovereignty. The fight for justice and reclamation of traditional lands is ongoing, as indigenous communities articulate their connection to the land and the need for sustainable practices that honor their heritage.

In conclusion, the pursuit of gold has wrought significant consequences on indigenous populations throughout history. From environmental destruction and displacement to socio-economic exploitation and cultural erosion, the legacy of gold exploration is complex and fraught with challenges. Recognizing this impact is essential for fostering a more equitable future, where indigenous voices and rights are respected in the context of gold mining and resource extraction. As the world grapples with the implications of its gold-driven past, the resilience and agency of indigenous communities remain crucial in shaping a sustainable and just future.

The Role of Gold in Colonial Economies

Gold has long been a symbol of wealth and power, and during the colonial era, its significance extended far beyond mere economic value. The quest for gold motivated European powers to expand their territories, develop new trade routes, and establish colonies across the globe. This pursuit fundamentally shaped the economic policies of colonial powers, influencing trade dynamics, labor systems, and the very fabric of societies in colonized regions.

The Economic Motivations Behind Colonization

In the 15th and 16th centuries, the Age of Exploration marked a pivotal point in history where European nations sought new sources of wealth to bolster their economies. The discovery of gold in the New World, particularly in regions such as present-day Mexico and Peru, fueled a frenzy among colonial powers, especially Spain. The influx of gold and silver from the Americas significantly enriched the Spanish crown, enabling it to finance wars in Europe and assert its dominance on the global stage. This wealth transformed Spain into one of the foremost powers of the time, fundamentally altering the balance of power in Europe.

Trade Routes and Mercantilism

The pursuit of gold shaped mercantilist policies, which emphasized the importance of accumulating precious metals to enhance national wealth. Colonial economies were structured around the extraction of gold and other resources, leading to the establishment of intricate trade networks. The triangular trade route exemplified this, as European powers transported gold, sugar, and tobacco from the Americas, slaves from Africa, and manufactured goods back to both regions. This system not only enriched colonial powers but also entrenched slavery and exploitation within colonial economies.

Labor Systems and the Gold Economy

The demand for gold necessitated a labor force capable of extracting and processing this coveted resource. Colonial powers resorted to various labor systems, including the encomienda system in Spanish America, where colonizers were granted the right to extract labor from Indigenous populations in exchange for protection and Christianization. This system often resulted in severe exploitation, leading to the decline of Indigenous populations due to overwork and introduced diseases. The extraction of gold thus became a brutal enterprise that not only enriched colonial powers but also decimated local communities and cultures.

The Impact on Indigenous Economies

The influx of gold and the subsequent colonial exploitation had profound effects on Indigenous economies. Traditional systems of trade and resource management were disrupted as European powers imposed their economic structures. Gold became a new standard of value, often displacing Indigenous currencies and trade practices. The introduction of European goods altered consumption patterns, leading to economic dependency on colonial powers. This shift undermined local economies and reinforced the subjugation of Indigenous peoples, who were often relegated to the margins of the new economic orders.

The Legacy of Gold in Colonial Economies
The legacy of gold in colonial economies is complex and multifaceted. While it fueled the growth of European empires and facilitated the rise of global trade networks, it also sowed the seeds of economic disparity and social injustice that persist in many regions today. The extraction of gold and the policies surrounding it created a cycle of wealth accumulation for colonial powers while perpetuating poverty and disenfranchisement for colonized peoples.

In conclusion, the role of gold in colonial economies was not merely a matter of resource extraction; it was a driving force behind the economic policies of colonial powers that reshaped the world. The quest for gold led to the establishment of oppressive labor systems, the disruption of Indigenous economies, and the creation of trade routes that transformed global interactions. This historical pursuit of wealth through gold has left a lasting impact on contemporary economic systems and social structures, underscoring the enduring legacy of colonialism in the modern world.

Gold and the Slave Trade: An Unspoken Connection

The transatlantic slave trade, which spanned from the 16th to the 19th centuries, was a dark chapter in human history, characterized by the forced transportation of millions of Africans to the Americas for labor. While the primary commodities involved in this trade were sugar, tobacco, and cotton, gold also played a crucial role, particularly as a symbol of wealth and a medium of exchange that facilitated the trade itself. The connection between gold mining and the transatlantic slave trade is complex and multifaceted, reflecting the interdependence of economies, power structures, and human suffering.

In the Americas, particularly in regions like Brazil and the Caribbean, gold mining became a significant industry that demanded a large workforce. The initial influx of enslaved Africans was driven by the labor shortages resulting from the brutal conditions and high mortality rates faced by Indigenous peoples, who were often the first labor source exploited by European colonizers. As gold mining expanded, so did the demand for enslaved labor, as European powers sought to maximize profits from their colonial ventures.

The Portuguese, Spanish, and later the British and French empires recognized the profitability of gold mining in the New World. In Brazil, for instance, the discovery of gold in the late 17th century led to a rush that transformed the economy. The gold mining regions, particularly in Minas Gerais, required a massive labor force. Enslaved Africans were forcibly transported to meet this demand, as their labor was deemed essential for extracting gold efficiently. It is estimated that a significant portion of the enslaved Africans brought to Brazil were used in gold mining operations, where they faced grueling conditions, long hours, and harsh treatment.

The wealth generated from gold mining was not only significant for the individual colonies but also for the European powers that controlled them. Gold became a critical component of the economies of colonial empires, allowing them to finance further expansion and military endeavors. The riches extracted from gold mines contributed to the economic foundation of the empires, which in turn perpetuated the cycle of exploitation through the slave trade. Gold served as a currency that facilitated trade, enabling the purchase of more enslaved individuals and the financing of colonial projects.

Moreover, the gold obtained through these mining operations was often used to buy goods that were traded in Europe and other markets. The triangular trade system, which connected Europe, Africa, and the Americas, relied on a network where gold and other resources were exchanged for enslaved individuals, creating a vicious cycle of exploitation and profit. As European nations competed for dominance in the New World, the interconnection between gold and the slave trade became more pronounced, as wealth accumulation through gold mining directly fueled the demand for additional enslaved labor.

The environmental and social consequences of this exploitation were profound. Gold mining operations often led to ecological degradation, disrupting local ecosystems and displacing communities. Additionally, the human cost of slavery was incalculable, with countless lives lost and families torn apart. The legacy of this exploitation continues to resonate today, as the impacts of colonialism and the slave trade still affect societies globally.

In conclusion, the link between gold mining and the transatlantic slave trade is an essential yet often overlooked aspect of both economic history and the narrative of human rights violations. Understanding this connection sheds light on the broader consequences of colonial exploitation and the enduring impacts of wealth disparities founded on the suffering of countless individuals. As we reflect on the history of gold, it is vital to recognize not only its allure and value but also the moral implications tied to its extraction and the human cost of its pursuit.

Chapter 6

Gold and the Development of Modern Economies

The Gold Standard: Birth of Modern Monetary Systems

The gold standard represents a pivotal moment in the history of global monetary systems, establishing a framework that linked currency values directly to gold. This method of valuing currency emerged in the 19th century and provided a basis for international trade, investment, and economic stability. Understanding how the gold standard came to be requires a look at its historical context, operational mechanics, and the implications it had for economies worldwide.

Historical Context

The rise of the gold standard can be traced back to the increasing need for a reliable medium of exchange following centuries of barter systems. By the late Middle Ages, gold and silver coins had become prevalent in Europe, serving as the primary currency for trade. However, the absence of standardized weights and measures led to confusion and mistrust. The necessity for a more stable and universally accepted currency prompted nations to adopt the gold standard.

In 1717, Sir Isaac Newton established the gold standard in Britain by setting the price of gold in terms of British currency. This act laid the groundwork for other countries to follow suit. The 19th century saw a significant shift as countries like France, Germany, and the United States began to formally adopt the gold standard. The culmination of this movement occurred at the end of the 19th century when a majority of industrialized nations embraced gold-backed currencies.

Operational Mechanics

Under the gold standard, currencies were directly tied to a specific amount of gold, which meant that governments had to hold gold reserves equivalent to the value of their currency in circulation. This system provided an automatic mechanism to regulate the money supply: if a country exported more than it imported, it would receive gold in exchange, increasing its monetary reserves and allowing for the issuance of more currency. Conversely, excessive currency printing would lead to a depletion of gold reserves, forcing governments to tighten monetary policy.

The gold standard facilitated international trade by creating a stable exchange rate regime. Because currencies were pegged to gold, foreign exchange rates were predictable, reducing the risks associated with international transactions. This predictability encouraged cross-border commerce and investment, fostering economic growth and globalization.

Implications for Economies
The gold standard had profound implications for global economies. It provided a sense of security and trust in currency, which was essential for economic stability. However, it also imposed significant constraints on monetary policy. Governments were limited in their ability to respond to economic crises, as they could not easily adjust the money supply without risking their gold reserves.

The interwar period and the Great Depression highlighted the vulnerabilities of the gold standard. As countries faced economic challenges, many resorted to abandoning the gold standard in favor of more flexible monetary systems. The United States officially left the gold standard in 1933, marking a significant turning point in global finance.

Legacy of the Gold Standard
The legacy of the gold standard can still be felt today. While most nations have moved to fiat currencies—where the value is not directly tied to physical commodities—the historical precedent set by the gold standard shaped the development of modern banking systems and monetary policies. It laid the groundwork for the establishment of international financial institutions and agreements that continue to govern global economics.

In conclusion, the gold standard was instrumental in shaping the birth of modern monetary systems. By linking currencies to gold, it provided a foundation for international trade and economic stability, while also revealing the limitations of rigid monetary systems. As the world continues to navigate the complexities of modern finance, the principles established during the era of the gold standard remain relevant, reminding us of the delicate balance between currency value, economic growth, and monetary policy.

Gold and Banking: The Rise of Financial Institutions
The relationship between gold and banking is deeply intertwined, with gold serving as a pivotal element in the development of modern financial institutions. This relationship can be traced back to ancient civilizations where gold was first used as a medium of exchange, a store of value, and a symbol of wealth. However, it was during the Middle Ages and the Renaissance that gold began to profoundly influence the evolution of banking systems, laying the groundwork for the complex financial institutions we rely on today.

The Role of Gold in Early Banking
In the early days of banking, particularly in medieval Europe, gold functioned as the principal basis for monetary transactions. Goldsmiths, who initially operated as custodians of gold, began to issue receipts for deposited gold. These receipts were more convenient for trade than the physical gold itself, as they could be easily exchanged. Over time, these receipts evolved into promissory notes, which were used as a form of currency. This innovation was crucial in establishing trust and facilitating trade, as individuals could conduct transactions without the constant need to handle physical gold.

As commerce expanded, the demand for reliable banking services grew. Goldsmiths began to take on more banking functions, lending money and accepting deposits. By holding gold reserves, banks could back the notes they issued, ensuring that the value of their currency remained stable. This practice of maintaining a gold reserve became fundamental to the concept of banking, as it provided a reliable standard against which the currency could be measured.

The Birth of the Gold Standard
The establishment of the gold standard in the 19th century marked a significant milestone in the relationship between gold and banking. Under the gold standard, the value of a nation's currency was directly linked to a specific amount of gold. This system provided stability to the monetary system, as it limited the ability of governments to print money beyond their gold reserves. Countries that adopted the gold standard experienced increased trade and investment, as it fostered a sense of financial security and predictability in international transactions.

Banks benefitted immensely from the gold standard, as it encouraged individuals and businesses to deposit their gold in banks for safekeeping. This led to the accumulation of substantial gold reserves, which banks could then use to extend credit, thereby fueling economic growth. The ability of banks to lend against these reserves allowed for the expansion of businesses, the development of infrastructure, and the facilitation of international trade.

The Decline of the Gold Standard and the Rise of Modern Banking
Despite its benefits, the gold standard faced significant challenges, particularly during times of economic crisis. The Great Depression of the 1930s highlighted the limitations of a gold-backed currency, leading many nations to abandon the gold standard in favor of fiat currencies—money that has value by government decree rather than backed by physical commodities. This transition marked a significant shift in the banking landscape, as financial institutions began to operate on a new foundation of credit and trust rather than gold reserves.

With the decline of the gold standard, banks gained greater flexibility in monetary policy, allowing for more dynamic responses to economic conditions. However, the legacy of gold in banking remains evident. Many central banks today still hold substantial gold reserves as a hedge against inflation and economic instability, reflecting gold's enduring status as a safe-haven asset.

Conclusion

The rise of banking institutions has been significantly influenced by the role of gold throughout history. From the early practices of goldsmiths to the establishment of the gold standard, and into the modern era of fiat currencies, gold has served as both a foundation and a stabilizing force for financial institutions. Today, while the direct link between gold and banking has diminished, the historical significance of gold in the development of banking systems continues to shape the financial landscape, reminding us of gold's timeless allure and its complex relationship with money and value.

The Role of Gold in Industrialization

The Industrial Revolution, which began in the late 18th century and continued into the 19th century, marked a period of profound transformation in economies, technologies, and societal structures. Gold played a significant yet often underappreciated role in this sweeping change, serving as a catalyst for industrial progress and economic expansion.

Financial Stability and Investment

At the heart of industrialization was the need for capital to fund burgeoning enterprises, infrastructure, and technological innovations. Gold, revered for its intrinsic value and stability, became a foundational element in establishing modern banking systems. As currencies began to adopt the gold standard—a monetary system in which currency value was directly linked to gold—financial institutions gained a reliable means of ensuring the value of their currencies. This stability encouraged both domestic and international investments in industrial ventures, as investors felt more secure in the value of their investments.

Facilitating Trade and Commerce

Gold's role extended beyond mere investment; it facilitated trade as nations began to engage in extensive commercial exchanges. The establishment of a gold standard simplified international trade relations by providing a universal measure of value. Merchants and traders could more easily conduct transactions across borders, knowing the equivalent value of their goods in gold. This increase in trade not only stimulated local economies but also created a demand for raw materials and manufactured goods, further driving the industrial engine.

Technological Advancements
As industries expanded, the demand for gold itself grew, particularly in new technological applications. Gold's exceptional conductivity and resistance to corrosion made it an essential material in early electrical technologies. Its use in telegraph systems and later in telephony was crucial in enhancing communication networks, which were indispensable for coordinating the logistics of industrial production and distribution. Moreover, gold's malleability allowed for intricate designs in machinery and instruments, underscoring its importance in engineering and scientific advancements.

Mining and Economic Development
The quest for gold also spurred exploration and mining, leading to the establishment of mining industries that not only produced gold but also created jobs and stimulated local economies. The development of mining technology, including innovations in extraction and refining processes, allowed for more efficient gold production. This created a ripple effect, as the wealth generated from gold mining funded further industrial activities, such as railroads and manufacturing facilities, thereby enhancing overall economic development.

The Global Gold Rush
The late 19th century witnessed significant gold rushes, notably in California and Australia, which attracted a massive influx of labor and capital. These events not only increased gold supply but also contributed to population growth and urbanization. Cities sprung up around mining operations, leading to the development of infrastructure, such as railroads and telegraph lines, which were critical for industrial logistics. The wealth acquired from these gold rushes was often reinvested into various industrial sectors, propelling advancements in technology and manufacturing.

Conclusion
In summary, gold's multifaceted role in the Industrial Revolution cannot be overstated. It provided financial stability, facilitated trade, and spurred technological advancements while simultaneously boosting local economies through mining activities. As a linchpin of emerging financial systems and a catalyst for industrial growth, gold was instrumental in shaping the modern economic landscape. Its legacy continues to influence contemporary financial practices and industrial strategies, highlighting its enduring significance in the history of human civilization.

The Global Gold Trade: From Mines to Markets
Gold has long held a revered status in human civilization, not just as a symbol of wealth and power but also as a critical economic commodity. The global gold trade is a complex system that

encompasses the extraction, processing, trading, and valuation of gold on an international scale. Understanding this intricate network provides insights into how gold continues to shape economies, cultures, and financial systems worldwide.

Extraction and Production

The journey of gold begins in the earth's crust, where it is often found in quartz veins, alluvial deposits, or as a byproduct of copper and other metal mining. Major gold-producing countries include China, Australia, Russia, the United States, and Canada, with each region employing various mining techniques—ranging from artisanal small-scale mining to large-scale industrial operations. The extraction process involves several stages, including exploration, extraction, refining, and smelting, all of which contribute to the final market-ready product.

Once mined, gold ore undergoes a refining process to remove impurities and achieve a high level of purity, typically 99.99% for investment-grade bullion. This refined gold is then transformed into bars, coins, or other forms suitable for trade. The London Bullion Market Association (LBMA) plays a crucial role in establishing standards for gold bars, ensuring that only gold of the highest quality enters the global market.

International Trade Networks

The international trade of gold is facilitated by a web of financial institutions, dealers, and exchanges. Major gold exchanges, such as the London Metal Exchange (LME) and the Shanghai Gold Exchange (SGE), serve as platforms for buying and selling gold. These exchanges provide a transparent mechanism for price discovery and trading, where spot prices are influenced by supply and demand dynamics, geopolitical events, and economic indicators such as inflation and currency fluctuations.

Gold is traded both physically, in the form of bullion, and as financial instruments, such as futures contracts and exchange-traded funds (ETFs). The latter have become increasingly popular, allowing investors to gain exposure to gold without the need to physically hold the metal. This dual nature of gold trading adds layers of complexity to its valuation.

Valuation Factors

The value of gold is determined by a multitude of factors. One of the most significant is the global economic climate; during times of economic uncertainty, gold often acts as a safe haven asset, driving up demand and, consequently, prices. Historical events, such as financial crises, wars, and political instability, have all led to spikes in gold prices as investors flock to the perceived security of gold.

Additionally, currency fluctuations, particularly the strength of the U.S. dollar, play a vital role in gold pricing. Since gold is typically priced in dollars, a weaker dollar can make gold cheaper for holders of foreign currencies, boosting demand and driving up prices. Conversely, stronger currencies can lead to a decline in gold prices.

Sustainability and Ethical Considerations
In recent years, the global gold trade has faced scrutiny regarding ethical mining practices and environmental impacts. Issues such as child labor, unsafe working conditions, and ecological degradation have prompted calls for more sustainable and responsible mining practices. Initiatives like the Responsible Gold Mining Principles (RGMP) seek to promote ethical practices within the industry, ensuring that gold is sourced responsibly and that its extraction does not come at the expense of local communities or the environment.

Conclusion
The global gold trade is a dynamic and multifaceted industry that reflects not only economic principles but also cultural values and ethical considerations. From the mines where gold is extracted to the markets where it is traded, the journey of gold is a testament to its enduring allure and significance in human society. As the world continues to evolve, so too will the systems and practices surrounding the trade of this precious metal, making it a focal point of economic activity and cultural identity for generations to come.

The Shift Away from the Gold Standard

The gold standard was a monetary system in which a country's currency or paper money had a value directly linked to gold. Countries adhering to this system agreed to convert currency into a fixed amount of gold and established gold reserves to back their currency issuance. This system provided a stable framework for international trade and exchange rates for much of the 19th and early 20th centuries. However, various economic, political, and social factors led to a gradual abandonment of the gold standard, culminating in its near-complete dissolution in the 20th century.

One primary reason for the shift away from the gold standard was the economic upheaval caused by World War I. The war effort required vast sums of money, leading governments to print more currency than they had gold reserves to back. This overextension resulted in inflationary pressures that undermined the stability the gold standard was supposed to provide. In the aftermath of the war, many countries faced economic instability and sought to manage their economies through more flexible monetary policies. This included the ability to print money in response to economic conditions, a capability severely limited under the constraints of the gold standard.

The Great Depression of the 1930s further exacerbated the flaws of the gold standard. As economic conditions worsened, countries found themselves trapped by the rigidities of gold backing. The inability to adjust currency supply to stimulate economies led to deflation and prolonged economic hardship. In response, nations began to abandon the gold standard in favor of more dynamic monetary policies. The United States, under President Franklin D. Roosevelt, officially left the gold standard in 1933, urging citizens to exchange their gold coins, gold bullion, and gold certificates for dollars and thus centralizing gold reserves in the hands of the government.

The Bretton Woods Conference in 1944 established a new international monetary order where the U.S. dollar became the world's primary reserve currency, convertible into gold at a fixed rate of $35 per ounce. This arrangement created a semi-gold standard, with other currencies pegged to the dollar rather than gold itself. However, as economic growth surged in the post-war period, the U.S. struggled to maintain gold reserves to back the increasing amount of dollars in circulation. By the late 1960s, the system faced immense pressure, as foreign nations began to exchange their dollars for gold, depleting U.S. reserves.

The culmination of these pressures came in 1971 when President Richard Nixon officially suspended the dollar's convertibility into gold, effectively ending the Bretton Woods system. This shift marked a significant transition to fiat currency systems, where money's value is not backed by physical commodities but rather by the government that issues it. The move allowed greater flexibility in monetary policy, enabling countries to respond more effectively to economic fluctuations without the constraints imposed by gold reserves.

The abandonment of the gold standard also reflected a broader ideological shift towards neoliberal economic policies throughout the late 20th century. Economists began to favor market-driven approaches to currency valuation, believing that the market could better determine the value of currencies based on supply and demand factors. This led to the widespread adoption of floating exchange rates, where currencies fluctuate against one another based on market forces rather than being fixed to gold or another commodity.

In conclusion, the transition away from the gold standard was driven by a complex interplay of economic crises, the need for flexible monetary policy, and the evolution of global economic thought. This shift allowed for more dynamic economic management and paved the way for the modern monetary systems we observe today, characterized by fiat currencies and the ability for governments to influence their economies through monetary policy. As a result, while gold remains a significant asset, its role as a foundation for national currencies has largely diminished.

Chapter 7

Gold in Art and Culture

Gold in Religious Art

Gold has held a profound significance in various religious traditions throughout history, occupying a central role in the creation of religious art, icons, and rituals. This precious metal, with its lustrous sheen and permanence, has often been viewed as a symbol of divine presence, purity, and eternal life. Its use in religious contexts can be traced back to ancient civilizations, where it was employed to honor deities, enhance sacred spaces, and convey the transcendental nature of spiritual beliefs.

Historical Context of Gold in Religious Art

From the earliest recorded civilizations, such as those in Mesopotamia and ancient Egypt, gold was utilized to craft intricate religious artifacts. In ancient Egypt, gold was not only a symbol of wealth but also a material believed to possess divine properties. The Egyptians adorned their temples and tombs with gold, crafting statues of gods and pharaohs, and using gold leaf to cover sacred objects. This application of gold signified the gods' majesty and the afterlife's splendor, encapsulating a belief that the divine could be visually represented through material beauty.

In addition to Egypt, gold played a significant role in the religious practices of cultures across the globe. In Mesoamerica, the Aztecs and Maya incorporated gold into their rituals, crafting ceremonial masks, jewelry, and offerings to appease their gods. The shimmering gold was thought to embody the sun's power, thus serving as a medium through which the divine could be approached.

Icons and Relics

In Christianity, gold has been similarly revered, particularly in the creation of icons and religious relics. The Byzantine Empire is famous for its use of gold in religious art, particularly in mosaics and icons. Artists used gold leaf to enhance the luminosity of saints' images, creating an ethereal quality that reflected the heavenly realm. These golden representations served not only as objects of beauty but also as conduits for prayer and devotion, allowing worshippers to connect with the divine.

Relics, or physical remains of saints, were often encased in gold and precious jewels to signify their sanctity and importance. The golden reliquaries housed within churches across Europe not only served as containers for these sacred objects but also as artistic masterpieces that conveyed the glory of the divine through their craftsmanship and opulence.

Ritualistic Use of Gold
Gold's role in religious rituals extends beyond mere decoration; it is often integral to the ceremonies themselves. In many cultures, gold is used in offerings and sacrifices, symbolizing the giver's devotion and reverence. For example, in Hinduism, gold is commonly used in puja (worship) rituals, where devotees present gold ornaments and currency to deities as expressions of gratitude and supplication.

Furthermore, gold is often associated with the concept of purification. In various religious traditions, it is believed that gold can cleanse and sanctify spaces and objects, making it an essential material in the construction of altars, temples, and sacred vessels. In Judaism, the Ark of the Covenant, which held the tablets of the Ten Commandments, was covered in gold to signify its holy contents and the divine presence it represented.

The Timeless Allure of Gold in Religion
The enduring allure of gold in religious art and practices can be attributed to its unique properties and the meanings ascribed to it by different cultures. Its resistance to tarnishing symbolizes immortality and the divine, while its brilliance captures the human imagination, signifying the transcendent. As societies evolve, the use of gold in religious contexts continues to reflect the complexities of faith, identity, and cultural heritage.

In summary, gold's application in religious art is a testament to its multifaceted significance across cultures and epochs. It serves as a bridge between the material and the spiritual, embodying humanity's quest for the divine and enduring reverence for the sacred. Whether as icons, relics, or integral components of rituals, gold remains a powerful symbol of faith, devotion, and the quest for connection with the transcendent.

The Use of Gold in Fine Art: From Ancient to Modern Times
Gold has held a prominent place in visual art throughout history, serving not only as a medium of aesthetic expression but also as a symbol of divine power, wealth, and transcendence. Its unique properties—luster, malleability, and resistance to tarnishing—have made it an ideal material for artists across cultures and epochs, leading to its incorporation in various forms of fine art, from sculpture and painting to decorative arts.

Ancient Civilizations and Religious Significance

In ancient civilizations, gold was often used in religious art and artifacts. The Egyptians, for instance, utilized gold extensively in tombs and temples, crafting intricate burial masks, jewelry, and offerings to the gods. The iconic funerary mask of Tutankhamun, made of gold and adorned with precious stones, exemplifies the artistic mastery and spiritual significance attributed to gold. It was believed that gold was the flesh of the gods, which imbued these objects with a divine quality intended to protect and guide the deceased in the afterlife.

Similarly, in Mesopotamia, gold was used to create religious idols and ceremonial objects. The intricate gold decorations found in the Royal Cemetery at Ur reflect the skill of ancient artisans and the importance of gold in religious practices. This trend continued in other cultures, such as in the Indus Valley and ancient China, where gold was used in rituals, artifacts, and ceremonial regalia, reinforcing its status as a medium linked to the divine.

Classical Antiquity and Artistic Mastery

During the Classical period, gold maintained its significance in art. In Greek culture, gold was employed in both architecture and sculpture, most notably in the gilded statues of gods and heroes. The statue of Athena Parthenos, crafted by Phidias, was made of gold and ivory, representing the pinnacle of artistic achievement in the ancient world. The use of gold leaf in painting also became prevalent, enhancing the luminosity of religious icons and decorative motifs.

In the Roman Empire, gold continued to play a vital role in art and culture. It was commonly used in mosaics, jewelry, and coins, showcasing the wealth and power of the empire. The use of gold in coinage allowed for a standardization of value that facilitated trade, but it also served as a canvas for artistic expression, with emperors commissioning coins adorned with intricate designs and portraits.

The Medieval and Renaissance Periods

The Middle Ages saw a shift in the use of gold in art, particularly in religious contexts. Illuminated manuscripts became a prominent artistic form, with gold leaf applied to pages to highlight scripture and illustrations. This practice not only demonstrated the wealth of the commissioning institutions, such as monasteries, but also conveyed the sacredness of the texts.

The Renaissance marked a revival of classical ideals, and gold re-emerged as a favored material among artists. Masters like Titian and Raphael incorporated gold leaf in their paintings to enhance the richness of their works. The opulence of gold was further utilized in altarpieces and sculptures, epitomizing the era's focus on beauty and the divine.

Modern Interpretations and Contemporary Art
In the modern era, artists have continued to explore gold's potential in new ways. From Gustav Klimt's lavish use of gold leaf in his paintings, such as "The Kiss," to contemporary artists like Anish Kapoor, who integrates gold in installations and sculptures, the allure of gold persists. Its association with luxury and status has made it a recurring theme in contemporary art, symbolizing both aspiration and critique of materialism.

Moreover, the revival of gold in modern art reflects broader conversations around identity, value, and cultural heritage. Artists utilize gold to challenge perceptions of wealth and to interrogate its implications in a globalized world.

Conclusion
From ancient to modern times, gold's role in fine art has been multifaceted, evolving with cultural values and technological advancements. Its enduring appeal lies not only in its physical properties but also in its rich symbolism, representing the intersection of beauty, power, and spirituality. As we continue to explore the intersection of art and material culture, gold remains a significant medium that shapes our understanding of human creativity and expression.

The Use of Gold in Jewelry: Status and Fashion
Gold has long held a significant place in human culture, particularly as a medium for adornment and expression in the form of jewelry. The use of gold in jewelry dates back thousands of years, and its evolution as a symbol of wealth and beauty reflects broader social, economic, and aesthetic trends throughout history. Today, gold jewelry is not only cherished for its aesthetic appeal but also for its cultural significance and status as a financial asset.

Historical Context
The earliest evidence of gold jewelry dates back to around 3000 BCE, with discoveries in ancient Egypt. The Egyptians crafted intricate gold artifacts, ranging from simple adornments to elaborate pieces meant for burial with pharaohs and nobles. Gold was associated with the divine and the afterlife, and its use in jewelry signified both wealth and a connection to the gods. The craftsmanship of jewelry evolved, showcasing techniques such as granulation, filigree, and inlay, which were used to enhance the beauty of gold.

In ancient Mesopotamia, gold jewelry played a crucial role in trade and personal adornment. The Sumerians and Akkadians fashioned gold into intricate pieces that symbolized power and affluence. Gold ornaments were often worn by both genders, reflecting a society where wealth was openly displayed. Similarly, in the Indus Valley civilization, gold jewelry was used not just as decoration but also as a form of currency, illustrating its dual role in society.

Cultural Significance

Throughout history, gold jewelry has been imbued with cultural significance, often representing social status, heritage, and identity. In many cultures, the act of wearing gold jewelry is intertwined with traditions and rituals. For example, in India, gold jewelry is an integral part of marriage ceremonies, symbolizing prosperity and good fortune for the bride. The gifting of gold, particularly in the form of intricate bangles and necklaces, is not only a matter of personal adornment but also a reflection of familial wealth and social standing.

In ancient Rome, gold became synonymous with power and prestige. The elite wore elaborate gold jewelry to signify their status, and this trend continued into the Byzantine Empire, where gold became a hallmark of nobility. During the Renaissance in Europe, gold jewelry experienced a revival, with artisans creating intricate pieces that combined gold with precious stones, reflecting the era's emphasis on artistry and individual expression.

Evolution in Design and Style

As societal norms shifted, so did the design and style of gold jewelry. The Victorian era saw the introduction of sentimental jewelry, where pieces were often adorned with intricate engravings and symbols of love and loss. The Art Nouveau movement of the late 19th and early 20th centuries emphasized organic forms and natural motifs, merging gold with enamel and gemstones in innovative ways.

In the modern era, gold jewelry continues to evolve, embracing contemporary designs that reflect current fashion trends. Minimalist aesthetics and sleek lines are popular, demonstrating that gold remains a versatile medium for self-expression. Additionally, the rise of ethical and sustainable practices in the gold industry has led to a growing demand for responsibly sourced gold jewelry, influencing designs that prioritize both beauty and environmental consciousness.

Conclusion

The use of gold in jewelry as a symbol of wealth and beauty is a testament to its enduring appeal across cultures and eras. From ancient artifacts to modern designs, gold jewelry reflects not only personal taste but also the complex interplay of social status, cultural heritage, and artistic innovation. As society continues to evolve, so too will the significance of gold jewelry, ensuring its place as a timeless emblem of beauty, wealth, and identity. Gold jewelry remains a powerful status symbol, a cherished form of adornment, and an integral part of human expression and history.

Gold in Literature and Myth: The Allure of the Precious Metal

Gold has long been a symbol of wealth, power, and divine favor in human culture, and this symbolism is richly reflected in literature and myth across various societies. From ancient texts to modern narratives, the portrayal of gold encapsulates its multifaceted allure, serving as both a coveted treasure and a harbinger of conflict, greed, and moral lessons.

In ancient mythology, gold is often associated with the gods and celestial realms. In Greek mythology, the golden fleece, coveted by Jason and the Argonauts, represents not just wealth but also the quest for honor and glory. This tale illustrates the dual nature of gold: it is both a tangible reward and a symbol of the trials one must endure to achieve greatness. Similarly, in Norse mythology, the gold obtained from the slain dragon Fafnir is not merely wealth; it is cursed, leading to betrayal and ruin. These narratives underscore a recurring theme: while gold is alluring, its pursuit can lead to moral corruption and destruction.

The myth of El Dorado, the fabled city of gold, is another potent example. Originating from the indigenous peoples of South America, this legend captivated European explorers in the 16th century. The allure of El Dorado was not just its purported wealth but also the embodiment of an unattainable ideal. It represented the ultimate quest for riches, driving men to extreme measures, often resulting in violence and exploitation. This myth highlights the psychological impact of gold, which transcends its material value, reflecting humanity's insatiable desire for more, regardless of the consequences.

In literature, gold frequently serves as a motif for the complexities of human desire. In Shakespeare's "The Merchant of Venice," the character Antonio's wealth is tied to gold, which becomes a focal point of conflict, particularly in the bond with Shylock. The story explores themes of mercy and justice, ultimately suggesting that the pursuit of wealth can lead to personal and societal dilemmas. Here, gold is not just a measure of wealth but also a catalyst for character development and ethical questioning.

Similarly, in J.R.R. Tolkien's "The Hobbit," the dragon Smaug hoards a vast treasure of gold, which symbolizes greed and destruction. The treasure, while powerful and enticing, brings strife to the dwarves and their surroundings, illustrating another literary theme: that gold can corrupt even the noblest intentions. The quest for gold thus becomes a journey fraught with peril and moral ambiguity, reflecting the timeless struggle between material wealth and ethical integrity.

In modern literature, gold continues to symbolize desire, ambition, and the costs of greed. Works like F. Scott Fitzgerald's "The Great Gatsby" use gold and wealth to critique the American

Dream, illustrating how the pursuit of wealth can lead to disillusionment and tragedy. Here, gold represents not only affluence but also the hollowness that often accompanies it, resonating with contemporary societal critiques of materialism.

The psychological appeal of gold extends beyond its physical properties; it embodies humanity's deepest aspirations and fears. It represents success, beauty, and security, while also serving as a cautionary tale about the perils of greed and the moral complexities of wealth. As a powerful symbol in literature and myth, gold continues to captivate our imagination, prompting reflections on our values, desires, and the impact of wealth on the human experience. Through these narratives, gold remains a timeless motif that encapsulates the allure and the inherent dangers of the pursuit of riches.

The Psychological Impact of Gold: Why We Value It

Gold has captivated the human imagination for millennia, not merely as a precious metal but as a symbol imbued with deeper psychological meanings. Its lasting appeal can be traced through various dimensions, including its aesthetic qualities, historical significance, cultural associations, and inherent characteristics. Understanding why we value gold requires an exploration of these intertwined factors that shape our perceptions and behaviors.

Aesthetic Allure

Gold's unique lustrous appearance immediately grabs attention. Its brilliant yellow hue, reflective qualities, and ability to resist tarnish make it visually appealing, leading to its use in jewelry, art, and decoration. This aesthetic quality is pivotal; humans are naturally drawn to beauty, and gold embodies a form of beauty that signifies success, wealth, and achievement. The psychological impact of its allure can be seen in how we adorn ourselves with gold jewelry, which not only enhances personal aesthetics but also serves as a statement of identity and status.

Historical Significance

Gold's historical role as a medium of exchange and a store of value has cemented its place in human culture. Societies have used gold as currency for thousands of years, establishing it as a standard of wealth. This historical context reinforces its value; the more entrenched gold is in human history, the more we perceive it as a reliable measure of worth. The psychological notion that "if something has endured through time, it must have inherent value" plays a crucial role in our perception of gold as a stable asset.

Cultural Associations

Across cultures, gold is often associated with divinity, power, and prosperity. Ancient civilizations revered gold as a gift from the gods, using it in religious artifacts and royal regalia. This cultural significance transfers to modern contexts, where gold is often linked to major life events such as weddings, anniversaries, and other milestones. The psychological impact of these associations cannot be underestimated; they create a narrative around gold that elevates its status beyond mere materialism to a symbol of love, commitment, and achievement.

Symbol of Security

In times of economic uncertainty, gold is perceived as a "safe haven" asset. The psychological need for security drives individuals to invest in gold when other investments seem risky. This behavior is deeply rooted in the fear of losing wealth and stability, prompting people to turn to gold as a tangible, enduring asset that can provide a sense of safety. The historical patterns of gold maintaining value during inflationary periods or economic downturns reinforce this belief, leading to a psychological reliance on gold as a protective measure against financial instability.

The Influence of Social Constructs

Gold also plays a significant role in social constructs surrounding wealth and success. Society often equates gold with affluence, leading to a psychological phenomenon where individuals aspire to obtain gold as a means of achieving social status. This aspiration can manifest in various ways, from acquiring gold jewelry to investing in gold bullion. The desire to own gold can become a driving force in people's lives, influencing lifestyle choices, financial decisions, and personal goals.

Conclusion

The psychological impact of gold is multifaceted, rooted in its aesthetic qualities, historical significance, cultural associations, and the security it provides. As a symbol of wealth, beauty, and stability, gold continues to hold a unique place in human society. Its enduring allure is not merely about its physical properties but rather the rich tapestry of meanings it has accumulated throughout history. Understanding this psychological dimension helps explain why gold remains a timeless and coveted element in our lives, transcending mere economic value to become a profound part of our cultural identity.

Chapter 8

Gold in Science and Technology

The Chemistry of Gold: What Makes It Unique?

Gold, with the chemical symbol Au (from the Latin 'aurum'), is a fascinating element that has captivated human interest for millennia. Its unique chemical properties not only contribute to its desirability as a precious metal but also dictate its various applications in technology, medicine, and industry. Understanding the chemistry of gold reveals why it holds such a prominent place in human history and culture.

Atomic Structure and Properties

Gold is classified as a transition metal, located in group 11 of the periodic table. It has an atomic number of 79, which means each atom of gold contains 79 protons and typically, 118 neutrons. Its atomic structure is characterized by a single electron in its outermost shell, which is responsible for many of its distinctive properties.

Gold is remarkably malleable and ductile; it can be hammered into extremely thin sheets (gold leaf) or drawn into fine wires without breaking. In fact, a single ounce of gold can be beaten into 300 square feet of gold leaf. This property arises from the strong metallic bonds between gold atoms, allowing them to slide past one another with relative ease.

Chemical Inertness

One of the most striking characteristics of gold is its chemical inertness. Gold does not react with most acids, bases, or other chemicals, which is why it does not tarnish or corrode over time—qualities that make it ideal for use in jewelry and for creating artifacts that last for centuries. This inertness is due to a stable electron configuration, which makes it resistant to oxidation and other chemical reactions that affect less noble metals.

However, gold can react with certain chemicals, such as aqua regia, a mixture of hydrochloric acid and nitric acid, which can dissolve gold. This property is utilized in refining processes where gold needs to be extracted from ores or recycled from electronic waste.

Alloys and Compounds

Gold can easily form alloys with other metals, such as silver, copper, and platinum, which modify its color, strength, and other characteristics. For example, the addition of copper creates red gold, while the addition of silver results in white gold. These alloys are significant in both jewelry making and industrial applications, allowing gold to be tailored for specific purposes.

In nature, gold is often found in its native state, but it can also form compounds, albeit less commonly than other metals. For instance, gold can form halides (like gold chloride) and complexes with other ligands, which are valuable in various chemical reactions and industrial processes.

Conductivity and Applications
Gold is an excellent conductor of electricity, which makes it indispensable in the electronics industry. Unlike copper or aluminum, gold does not corrode, ensuring long-lasting connections in electronic components. Its use in high-end connectors, switches, and circuit boards highlights its unique combination of conductivity and chemical stability.

Moreover, the biocompatibility of gold makes it suitable for medical applications. Nanoparticles of gold are increasingly used in drug delivery systems, diagnostics, and imaging techniques due to their unique optical properties and minimal toxicity.

Conclusion
The chemistry of gold is defined by its unique atomic structure, chemical inertness, malleability, and conductivity. These properties not only contribute to its enduring allure as a precious metal but also enable diverse applications across various fields, from jewelry to electronics and medicine. As our understanding of gold's chemistry continues to evolve, its role in technology and culture is likely to expand, maintaining its status as a symbol of wealth and a crucial resource in modern society.

Gold in Medicine: Historical and Modern Uses
Gold has long fascinated humanity, not only for its beauty and value but also for its unique properties that have made it a part of various medical practices throughout history. From ancient civilizations to contemporary medicine, gold has been employed in a multitude of ways, reflecting its versatility and enduring appeal.

Ancient Uses of Gold in Medicine
The medicinal use of gold dates back thousands of years, with records indicating its application in various cultures. Ancient Egyptians utilized gold in the embalming process, believing it had protective and preservative qualities. Gold was often used in amulets and talismans, as it was thought to hold magical properties that could ward off diseases and bring about healing.

In traditional Chinese medicine, gold was used to treat a range of ailments, including skin diseases and internal disorders. The ancient texts describe the use of gold leaf, which was ingested or applied topically, as a way of restoring health. This practice was rooted in the belief that gold could harmonize the body's energies and promote overall well-being.

The Greeks and Romans also recognized gold's therapeutic potential. The famous physician Hippocrates referenced the use of gold in treating wounds and skin conditions, while Pliny the Elder documented its application in various ointments and remedies. Gold compounds were believed to have anti-inflammatory properties, and physicians often prescribed them for joint pain and other ailments.

The Rise of Gold Compounds in Medicine

As medical knowledge evolved, the 19th century saw a significant advancement in the use of gold in therapeutic contexts. Gold salts, particularly gold sodium thiomalate, began to be used in the treatment of rheumatoid arthritis. Physicians observed that gold compounds could reduce inflammation and slow the progression of the disease. This marked the beginning of a more scientific approach to gold in medicine, as clinical studies began to validate its efficacy.

Gold therapy remained a popular treatment for rheumatoid arthritis well into the 20th century. While its use has declined with the advent of newer, more effective medications, gold compounds are still occasionally prescribed in cases where patients do not respond to other treatments.

Modern Applications of Gold in Medicine

In contemporary medicine, gold's unique properties have been harnessed in various innovative ways. One of the most significant advancements is in the field of diagnostics and targeted therapies. Nanoparticles of gold are being explored for their potential in imaging and drug delivery systems. Gold nanoparticles can be engineered to attach to specific cells or tissues, allowing for targeted treatment of diseases, including cancer. Their ability to absorb light makes them valuable in photothermal therapy, where localized heating can destroy cancer cells without harming surrounding healthy tissue.

Additionally, gold is used in certain medical devices, particularly in dentistry and orthopedic applications. Gold's biocompatibility and resistance to corrosion make it an ideal material for dental crowns, bridges, and implants. Its use in these applications ensures longevity and reduces the risk of allergic reactions.

Future Directions
The potential for gold in medicine continues to expand, with ongoing research into its role in regenerative medicine and immunotherapy. Scientists are investigating how gold nanoparticles can enhance the delivery of vaccines and improve immune responses against various diseases.

In conclusion, gold's journey through the annals of medicine reflects humanity's quest for healing and understanding. From ancient talismans to modern nanoparticles, gold has maintained its status as a valuable asset in medical treatment. As researchers explore its capabilities further, gold's legacy in medicine is likely to evolve, offering new possibilities for health and healing in the future.

The Role of Gold in Electronics and Industry
Gold, a highly coveted precious metal, has found a crucial place in modern technology and industry due to its unique physical and chemical properties. Renowned for its excellent conductivity, resistance to corrosion, and malleability, gold plays a pivotal role in numerous electronic applications, making it indispensable in the realm of contemporary electronics.

Electrical Conductivity
One of the primary attributes of gold that enhances its functionality in electronics is its superior electrical conductivity. Gold is an exceptional conductor of electricity, second only to silver. This quality ensures minimal electrical resistance, which is vital in the performance of electronic components. In the manufacturing of integrated circuits, gold is often used for wire bonding, where thin gold wires connect the semiconductor chip to the external circuitry. This application allows for reliable signal transmission and contributes to the longevity and efficiency of electronic devices.

Corrosion Resistance
In addition to its conductivity, gold's remarkable resistance to tarnish and corrosion makes it ideal for use in electronics. Unlike other metals that may oxidize or corrode over time, gold maintains its luster and conductivity, ensuring the longevity of electronic components. This property is particularly important in high-performance environments, such as aerospace and military applications, where reliability is paramount. Gold is commonly used in connectors, switches, and other components that require durable, corrosion-resistant materials to withstand harsh conditions.

Use in Modern Electronics
The application of gold in electronics extends beyond basic wiring and connectors. It is an essential material in the production of various advanced technologies, including smartphones, computers, and medical devices. In smartphones, for instance, gold is utilized in the connectors and circuit boards, contributing to the functionality of touch screens and cameras. Similarly, in

computers, gold is found in the internal components, enhancing the reliability of data transmission and processing.

Moreover, the rise of the Internet of Things (IoT) and smart devices has further amplified the demand for gold. As devices become more interconnected and reliant on seamless communication, the need for high-quality materials that can ensure efficient performance has surged. Gold's properties align perfectly with these requirements, making it a staple in the manufacturing of sensors, microprocessors, and other critical components.

Innovations in Gold Usage
The advancement of technology has also led to innovative applications of gold beyond traditional electronics. In recent years, researchers have explored the use of gold nanoparticles in various fields, including medicine and environmental science. Gold nanoparticles exhibit unique optical and electronic properties, enabling their use in targeted drug delivery systems and cancer treatments. Additionally, they are being investigated for environmental applications, such as pollution detection and remediation.

Economic Implications and Sustainability
While gold's functionality in electronics is unmatched, its procurement and use raise important economic and environmental considerations. The mining and refining of gold can have significant ecological impacts, prompting the industry to seek more sustainable practices. Innovations in gold recycling have emerged as a viable solution, allowing for the recovery and reuse of gold from electronic waste. This not only mitigates environmental damage but also reduces the demand for newly mined gold, contributing to a more sustainable future.

Conclusion
In summary, gold's role in electronics and industry is multifaceted, encompassing its use in essential components, advanced technologies, and innovative applications. Its unique properties—superior conductivity, corrosion resistance, and malleability—make it indispensable in modern electronics. As the industry moves toward more sustainable practices, gold will continue to be a key player in shaping the future of technology, balancing the demands of innovation with the need for environmental stewardship. The enduring significance of gold in electronics not only underscores its historical value but also hints at its promising future in an ever-evolving technological landscape.

Innovations in Gold Extraction and Refining
The quest for gold has been integral to human civilization, driving exploration, trade, and technological innovation. Over the centuries, gold extraction and refining methods have evolved significantly, influenced by advancements in technology and a deeper understanding of metallurgy. This section explores the critical innovations that have transformed the processes of

gold extraction and refining, enhancing efficiency, reducing environmental impact, and improving overall yield.

1. Advanced Mining Techniques

In the past, gold mining relied heavily on manual labor and rudimentary tools, often leading to inefficient extraction processes. Modern mining techniques, however, have revolutionized the industry. The introduction of mechanized equipment, such as excavators, bulldozers, and automated drilling systems, has significantly increased the scale of operations. These machines allow for the extraction of gold from deeper deposits, which were previously inaccessible, thus expanding the potential resources available for mining.

Additionally, innovations such as heap leaching have transformed the way low-grade ores are processed. In heap leaching, crushed ore is piled into heaps and treated with a leaching solution, typically cyanide, which dissolves the gold. This method is particularly effective for extracting gold from low-grade ores, making previously uneconomical deposits viable for mining.

2. Hydrometallurgy and Bioleaching

Hydrometallurgy has emerged as a potent alternative to traditional pyrometallurgical processes, which involve high-temperature smelting. The hydrometallurgical process utilizes aqueous solutions to extract metals from ores. This method can be more environmentally friendly, as it often requires less energy and produces fewer emissions.

Bioleaching, a subset of hydrometallurgy, employs microorganisms to facilitate the extraction of gold from ores. Certain bacteria can oxidize sulfide minerals, thereby liberating gold particles. This method is gaining traction due to its lower environmental impact and its ability to process complex ores that are resistant to conventional extraction methods.

3. Refining Technologies

Once gold is extracted, refining is necessary to achieve the high purity levels required for commercial use. Traditional methods such as cupellation, where lead is used to separate gold from ore, are being supplemented by more sophisticated technologies. The Miller process, which involves blowing chlorine gas through molten gold, allows for the rapid purification of gold to 99.5% purity. This process, while effective, can produce toxic waste products.

The Wohlwill process offers an alternative for achieving even higher purity levels (up to 99.99%). This electrochemical method involves dissolving impure gold in an electrolytic solution and depositing pure gold onto cathodes. Innovations in electrolytic refining equipment have improved the efficiency and safety of this process, allowing for more energy-efficient operations and minimizing the risk of hazardous material exposure.

4. Environmental Considerations

As awareness of the environmental impacts of mining has grown, so too have innovations aimed at minimizing harm. Technologies that focus on reducing water usage, such as closed-loop water systems, significantly lower the amount of freshwater consumed in mining operations. Additionally, advancements in waste management, including the development of more effective tailings management systems, are crucial in preventing contamination of local ecosystems.

Furthermore, the rise of sustainable mining practices is prompting companies to adopt innovations that prioritize ecological stewardship. For instance, the use of non-toxic reagents in place of harmful chemicals like cyanide is becoming more common, driven by both regulatory pressure and consumer demand for environmentally responsible practices.

5. Future Directions

Looking ahead, the future of gold extraction and refining will likely be shaped by continued technological advancements, including the potential for artificial intelligence and machine learning to optimize mining operations. These technologies can analyze vast amounts of data to improve resource management, predict ore quality, and enhance operational efficiency.

In conclusion, innovations in gold extraction and refining have not only improved yields and efficiencies but also addressed significant environmental challenges associated with gold mining. As technology evolves, the gold industry is poised to become more sustainable and economically viable, ensuring that gold continues to be a valuable resource for generations to come.

The Future of Gold in Emerging Technologies

As we move deeper into the 21st century, gold continues to assert its relevance beyond traditional uses in jewelry and finance. Its unique physical and chemical properties are paving the way for innovative applications in various cutting-edge technologies, including electronics, medicine, nanotechnology, and renewable energy.

One of the most significant emerging uses of gold is in the field of electronics. Gold is a superb conductor of electricity and is highly resistant to corrosion, making it an ideal material for electrical connectors, circuit boards, and microchips. As the demand for smaller, more efficient electronic devices grows, the need for materials that can perform at high levels while maintaining durability becomes critical. Recent advancements in microfabrication techniques have allowed for the production of ultra-thin gold films used in flexible electronics, wearables, and even smart textiles. These innovations not only improve device performance but also open avenues for more sustainable production methods, as gold's recyclability can mitigate electronic waste.

In the medical field, gold nanoparticles are gaining traction for their applications in diagnostics and targeted drug delivery systems. The biocompatibility of gold allows it to be used safely within the human body, and its unique optical properties enable it to function as a contrast agent in imaging technologies. For example, gold nanoparticles can be utilized in photothermal therapy, where they are directed to cancer cells and heated using light, effectively destroying tumors while minimizing damage to surrounding healthy tissues. Additionally, researchers are exploring gold's potential in immunotherapy, where its ability to enhance immune responses could lead to more effective cancer treatments.

Nanotechnology, which manipulates matter at the atomic and molecular scale, is another frontier where gold is making significant inroads. Gold nanostructures exhibit unique optical, electronic, and catalytic properties that render them valuable in various applications, from sensors to environmental remediation. For instance, gold nanoparticles can be engineered to detect specific biomolecules at extremely low concentrations, making them crucial for early disease diagnosis. Furthermore, their catalytic properties can be harnessed for the breakdown of pollutants, positioning gold as a key player in addressing environmental challenges.

Another promising area is the potential role of gold in renewable energy technologies. With the global push towards sustainable energy solutions, gold's properties may be beneficial in the development of advanced solar cells. For example, integrating gold nanoparticles into photovoltaic materials can increase energy conversion efficiency by improving light absorption. Researchers are also exploring the use of gold in hydrogen production through electrolysis, where gold catalysts could enhance the efficiency of splitting water into hydrogen and oxygen, a crucial step in hydrogen fuel production.

Lastly, as artificial intelligence (AI) continues to revolutionize industries, gold mining and exploration are not exempt from its influence. AI algorithms can analyze vast datasets to identify potential gold reserves more efficiently, reducing the environmental impact of exploratory drilling. Moreover, the integration of AI in gold refining processes can optimize operations, increasing yield while minimizing waste.

In conclusion, the future of gold in emerging technologies is bright and multifaceted. From electronics and medicine to nanotechnology and renewable energy, gold's inherent properties are being harnessed in innovative ways that promise to enhance our technological landscape while also addressing pressing global challenges. As research progresses and new applications are discovered, gold is set to remain a vital element in shaping the future, ensuring its legacy endures in the realms of science and technology.

Chapter 9

Gold in Global Politics and Diplomacy

Gold as a Tool of Diplomacy

Throughout history, gold has served not only as a medium of exchange and a store of value but also as a significant tool of diplomacy. Its intrinsic value and universal appeal have made it a powerful instrument in international relations, often used to forge alliances, settle disputes, and exhibit power. This section explores historical instances where gold played a crucial role in diplomatic efforts across various cultures and epochs.

One of the earliest examples of gold as a diplomatic tool can be traced back to ancient Egypt. Pharaohs utilized gold extensively in their relations with neighboring states, often as gifts or tributes to secure loyalty and foster alliances. Gold presented to foreign dignitaries symbolized both wealth and the divine right to rule, reinforcing the pharaoh's status and influence. For instance, during the reign of Pharaoh Hatshepsut, expeditions to the Land of Punt yielded not only gold but also exotic goods that were used to strengthen diplomatic ties with this distant kingdom.

In the context of the Roman Empire, gold was similarly employed as a diplomatic instrument. Emperors often used gold coins, known as aurei, to pay for military alliances or to bribe influential figures in conquered territories. This practice facilitated the expansion of Roman influence and control, as well as the stabilization of newly acquired regions. The use of gold in diplomacy was not merely transactional; it also served to project the might of Rome and reinforce the loyalty of its allies through the promise of wealth.

The Middle Ages saw a continuation of gold's diplomatic significance, particularly through royal marriages. Dynasties often exchanged large sums of gold as part of marriage agreements, effectively using it to cement alliances between powerful families. The dowries paid in gold were not only a symbol of wealth but also a strategic maneuver to secure political stability. For example, the marriage between Eleanor of Aquitaine and Henry II of England involved substantial gold dowries that helped consolidate their power in Europe.

As global exploration intensified during the Age of Exploration, gold became an essential commodity in diplomatic negotiations between European powers and indigenous populations.

Conquistadors, driven by the allure of gold, often utilized it as a bargaining chip in their dealings with Native American tribes. The promise of gold influenced treaties and alliances, albeit often under coercive circumstances. The Spanish crown, for instance, used gold acquired from the New World to fund its military campaigns and diplomatic endeavors in Europe, showcasing how gold was pivotal in international relations during this period.

In the modern era, gold has continued to play a crucial role in diplomacy, particularly in the formation of international agreements and economic treaties. The establishment of the Gold Standard in the 19th century exemplifies this trend, as nations pegged their currencies to gold to stabilize economies and facilitate trade. This created a system where gold reserves became a symbol of a nation's economic strength and diplomatic credibility, influencing relationships between countries.

Moreover, the strategic stockpiling of gold reserves by nations has often served as a deterrent against potential aggressors. Countries with substantial gold reserves can project economic stability, thereby enhancing their diplomatic standing on the global stage. This phenomenon can be seen in the post-World War II era, where nations rebuilt their economies and sought to reestablish diplomatic relations through gold-backed currencies and trade agreements.

In conclusion, gold has historically been a potent tool of diplomacy, facilitating alliances and shaping international relations across cultures and epochs. From ancient Egypt to modern economic treaties, the use of gold has underscored its significance not only as a commodity but also as a critical element in the art of diplomacy. The enduring allure of gold in international relations reflects its unique ability to bridge cultures, symbolize power, and foster cooperation among nations.

Gold and War: Financing Conflict

Gold has long served as a tangible measure of wealth, power, and authority, making it a pivotal asset in financing wars and conflicts throughout history. Its unique properties—scarcity, durability, divisibility, and portability—have established gold as a preferred medium for trade and a secure store of value. In times of war, the strategic importance of gold becomes magnified, as nations and empires seek to fund military campaigns, procure resources, and maintain economic stability.

Historically, gold has played a crucial role in facilitating the financing of wars. For instance, during the Roman Empire, gold coins known as aurei were minted to pay soldiers and fund military expeditions. The ability to produce and control gold currency allowed Rome to project power across vast territories, making it easier to recruit and maintain a formidable military force. Gold was not just a means of payment; it symbolized the might of the empire, reinforcing loyalty among troops and citizens alike.

In medieval Europe, the financing of wars often relied heavily on gold reserves. Monarchs would hoard gold to ensure they had the liquidity necessary to support military endeavors. The Hundred Years' War between England and France exemplifies this reliance on gold as both kingdoms sought to finance their armies through taxation and the accumulation of gold. As each side faced increasing financial strain, the need for gold became even more pressing, leading to the establishment of systems that allowed for the direct taxation of subjects to fund warfare.

The discovery of the New World in the 15th and 16th centuries further transformed the role of gold in warfare. The Spanish Conquistadors, driven by the pursuit of gold, financed their expeditions through the wealth they extracted from indigenous empires such as the Aztecs and Incas. This influx of gold not only enriched Spain but also allowed it to become a dominant military power in Europe. The Spanish crown used this newfound wealth to fund wars against rivals like France and England, illustrating how the quest for gold directly influenced the balance of power in Europe.

In the 19th and 20th centuries, gold continued to be a critical asset in financing conflicts. During World War I, nations turned to gold reserves to back war bonds, allowing them to raise significant funds from citizens willing to invest in their countries' military efforts. The gold standard, which linked currency values to gold, further entrenched gold's role in wartime economies, as countries sought to maintain their gold reserves to support their currencies and ensure economic stability during tumultuous times.

The relationship between gold and war is not solely economic but also deeply intertwined with political dynamics. Governments have historically used gold to forge alliances and secure loyalty from other nations. For instance, during World War II, the Allies and Axis powers sought to control gold reserves in occupied territories, recognizing their strategic importance in sustaining military campaigns and economies.

Today, while the nature of warfare has evolved, gold remains a relevant asset in conflict scenarios. Countries still regard gold as a safe haven during economic crises, often stockpiling gold to safeguard national wealth. In contemporary conflicts, illicit gold mining and trade have emerged as significant issues, with rebel groups and warlords exploiting gold resources to fund their operations, perpetuating cycles of violence and instability.

In conclusion, gold has been a fundamental aspect of financing wars and conflicts throughout history. Its enduring value as a medium of exchange and a store of wealth continues to influence military strategies and economic policies in the modern world. As nations navigate the complexities of warfare and economic stability, gold remains a powerful symbol of wealth, authority, and the lengths to which societies will go to secure their interests in times of conflict.

Gold Reserves and National Security

Gold has long been recognized as a symbol of wealth and economic stability. Its unique properties, combined with its historical significance, have made it a crucial asset for nations seeking to secure their economies. Gold reserves serve not only as a financial cushion but also as a strategic instrument in international relations, impacting national security.

Historical Context

The importance of gold reserves can be traced back to ancient civilizations, where gold was used as a medium of exchange and a store of value. As economies evolved, countries began to accumulate gold to back their currencies, particularly during the gold standard era. This system linked the value of currency directly to a specified amount of gold, providing a sense of stability and trust in the monetary system. Although most countries abandoned the gold standard in the 20th century, the significance of gold reserves has endured.

Economic Stability

Gold reserves play a pivotal role in ensuring economic stability. In times of financial crisis or inflation, gold serves as a safe haven asset. Unlike fiat currency, which can be devalued by government policies or economic mismanagement, gold generally retains its value over time. Nations with substantial gold reserves can reassure investors and the public about their economic stability, creating a buffer against market volatility. This stability can be crucial for maintaining confidence in a country's financial system, particularly during periods of uncertainty.

National Security Considerations

From a national security perspective, gold reserves are integral to a country's financial sovereignty. They act as a safeguard against external economic pressures, such as sanctions or trade disputes. For instance, countries facing sanctions may find their access to international financial systems restricted. In such scenarios, gold can be liquidated or used as collateral in transactions, allowing nations to navigate through economic isolation.

Moreover, gold reserves can also enhance a nation's bargaining power in international negotiations. Countries with significant gold holdings may leverage their reserves in diplomatic discussions, using them as a tool for securing favorable trade agreements or improving their global standing. This capacity to project economic strength can deter potential adversaries, contributing to a nation's overall security strategy.

Modern Perspectives

In contemporary times, many countries are revisiting the importance of gold in their monetary policies. Central banks are increasing their gold holdings as a hedge against currency fluctuations and geopolitical tensions. For instance, nations like Russia and China have actively sought to bolster their gold reserves, reflecting a strategic shift towards asset diversification. These countries view gold not just as a financial asset, but as a critical component of their national security strategy.

Challenges and Critiques

While gold reserves offer several benefits, they are not without challenges. The costs associated with maintaining and securing gold reserves can be significant. Additionally, the opportunity cost of holding vast amounts of gold—funds that could be invested elsewhere—poses a dilemma for some governments. Critics argue that excessive focus on gold can detract from investments in more productive assets, such as infrastructure or technology.

Conclusion

In conclusion, gold reserves continue to play an essential role in the economic and security frameworks of nations around the world. By providing a safeguard against economic instability and a means of enhancing geopolitical power, gold remains a cornerstone of national security strategies. As countries navigate an increasingly complex and unpredictable global landscape, the enduring appeal of gold as a secure asset is likely to persist, shaping the policies and strategies of nations for years to come.

The Politics of Gold Mining: Power, Corruption, and Control

Gold has long been associated with wealth and power, its allure drawing nations and individuals alike into a complex web of political dynamics. The politics of gold mining is a multifaceted issue that intertwines economic interests, environmental concerns, and social justice, often leading to corruption and conflict.

Economic Interests and Political Power

In many countries, especially those rich in natural resources, gold mining serves as a significant economic driver. Nations depend on gold extraction as it often constitutes a substantial portion of their GDP, foreign exchange earnings, and tax revenues. This economic dependence can lead to a concentration of power among political elites who control mining rights and licenses, sometimes resulting in policies that favor short-term profits over sustainable development.

For instance, in several African nations, gold mining has been linked to the perpetuation of authoritarian regimes. Government officials may establish monopolies over mining operations, using state resources to secure lucrative contracts with multinational corporations. These arrangements often sideline local communities and exacerbate inequalities, creating a landscape where wealth is concentrated at the top while the broader populace remains impoverished.

Corruption and Governance Issues

The gold mining sector is notoriously susceptible to corruption. The immense profits generated by gold can lead to bribery, embezzlement, and collusion between government officials and mining companies. In many instances, local communities find themselves powerless against these corrupt practices, which can manifest in the form of land grabs, environmental degradation, and the erosion of social and political structures.

For example, in countries like the Democratic Republic of Congo (DRC), the mining industry has been plagued by corruption and mismanagement. Gold mining operations have funded armed conflict, with various factions competing for control over valuable resources. This has resulted in a cycle of violence and instability, further complicating efforts to establish effective governance and the rule of law.

Environmental and Social Justice

The political dynamics of gold mining extend beyond economic and governance issues. Environmental degradation is a critical concern, as mining operations often lead to deforestation, water contamination, and loss of biodiversity. The extraction process itself can involve toxic chemicals, such as cyanide and mercury, posing significant health risks to local populations.

As awareness of these environmental impacts grows, social movements advocating for environmental justice are emerging, demanding accountability and sustainable practices from both governments and corporations. In many cases, these movements face repression, as the political elites seek to maintain control over lucrative mining operations. Activists campaigning for the rights of indigenous and local communities often find themselves targeted, leading to human rights abuses and violent crackdowns.

International Dimensions and Global Supply Chains

The politics of gold mining is not confined to national borders. The global demand for gold fuels an international market that can exacerbate local tensions. Multinational corporations often exploit lax regulations in developing countries, where they can operate with fewer restrictions compared to their home countries. This dynamic can perpetuate a cycle of exploitation, where local communities receive minimal benefits from the wealth generated by their land.

Moreover, the rise of ethical consumerism has prompted some companies to adopt responsible sourcing policies. However, the effectiveness of these initiatives varies widely, and ensuring transparency in gold supply chains remains a significant challenge. As consumers demand more ethically sourced products, the political implications of gold mining will continue to evolve, necessitating ongoing dialogue and reform.

Conclusion

The politics of gold mining is a complex interplay of economic interests, power dynamics, and social justice issues. As gold continues to symbolize wealth and status, its extraction will inevitably be entwined with the politics of the regions from which it is sourced. Addressing these challenges requires a concerted effort from governments, corporations, and civil society to promote transparency, accountability, and sustainable practices, ensuring that the benefits of gold mining are shared equitably among all stakeholders.

International Gold Agreements: Cooperation and Conflict

Throughout history, gold has stood as a symbol of wealth, power, and stability. Its intrinsic value has led to various international agreements and disputes, reflecting the complex dynamics between nations as they navigate the significance of this precious metal. International gold agreements have been crucial in shaping economic policies, trade relationships, and diplomatic ties, as countries have sought to manage their gold reserves and the global gold market.

One of the earliest examples of international cooperation regarding gold can be traced back to the establishment of the Gold Standard in the 19th century. Countries adopted this monetary system to stabilize their currencies by pegging them to a fixed quantity of gold. The Gold Standard aimed to facilitate international trade by providing a reliable and consistent measure of value. This system fostered economic stability among nations, as it limited inflation and encouraged fiscal responsibility. However, the reliance on gold also created tensions, particularly during periods of economic strain. As countries struggled with gold supply shortages, they often resorted to protectionist policies, leading to conflicts over access to gold mines and markets.

The Bretton Woods Agreement established in 1944 marked another significant moment in international gold cooperation. Under this system, the U.S. dollar was pegged to gold, while other currencies were pegged to the dollar. This arrangement aimed to promote global economic stability post-World War II and facilitated international trade. However, the growing imbalance between the U.S. dollar supply and gold reserves ultimately led to the collapse of the Bretton Woods system in the early 1970s. The subsequent abandonment of the gold standard by many countries ushered in an era of fiat currencies, leading to new dynamics in international gold agreements.

As the gold market evolved, so too did the nature of international agreements surrounding gold. The late 20th and early 21st centuries saw increased cooperation through organizations like the International Monetary Fund (IMF), which established mechanisms for gold sales and loans among member countries. The IMF's gold sales, particularly during the late 1990s, were aimed at supporting its financial stability and managing global economic crises. These coordinated efforts demonstrated how countries could work together to alleviate financial pressures while leveraging gold's value.

However, the quest for gold has also led to conflicts and disputes among nations. The competition for gold resources often triggers geopolitical tensions, especially in regions rich in gold deposits. For instance, the discovery of gold in South Africa during the late 19th century sparked conflicts over land rights and labor exploitation, leading to significant social and political upheaval. Similarly, the Gold Rushes in the United States and Australia resulted in violent confrontations between settlers and Indigenous populations, as the allure of gold led to land dispossession and cultural degradation.

In contemporary contexts, international gold agreements have also been influenced by issues such as environmental sustainability and ethical mining practices. The rise of consumer awareness about the environmental and social impacts of gold mining has prompted countries and organizations to establish frameworks that promote responsible sourcing and sustainable practices. Initiatives like the OECD Due Diligence Guidance for Responsible Supply Chains aim to mitigate the negative impacts of gold mining while promoting cooperation among nations to ensure ethical gold trade.

In conclusion, international gold agreements reflect a complex interplay of cooperation and conflict, driven by the enduring significance of gold in global economics and politics. As countries navigate the challenges of the gold market, the need for collaboration remains crucial in addressing issues related to trade, environmental sustainability, and ethical practices. Understanding this intricate landscape is essential for comprehending the future of gold in international relations and the broader implications for global economics.

Chapter 10

The Environmental Impact of Gold Mining

The Ecological Footprint of Gold Mining

Gold mining, while a significant contributor to global economies, carries a profound ecological footprint that impacts both the environment and local communities. The processes of extraction and refinement can result in extensive degradation of ecosystems, loss of biodiversity, and long-term environmental consequences. Understanding the ecological footprint of gold mining involves examining several key factors: land disruption, water pollution, energy consumption, and the broader implications for climate change.

Land Disruption and Habitat Loss

The initial phase of gold mining often involves clearing vast areas of land, which can lead to significant habitat destruction. Open-pit mining, one of the most common methods for extracting gold, requires extensive clearing of forests, grasslands, and other natural habitats. This disruption not only eliminates local flora and fauna but can also lead to soil erosion, which further exacerbates habitat loss. The alteration of landscapes can have cascading effects on local ecosystems, diminishing biodiversity and destabilizing food chains. In regions where indigenous communities depend on these ecosystems for their livelihoods, the impacts can be particularly severe, leading to social and economic dislocation.

Water Pollution

Gold mining operations frequently generate substantial amounts of waste, including toxic chemicals such as cyanide and mercury, which are used in the extraction process. When these substances enter water systems, they can contaminate rivers, lakes, and groundwater, posing significant risks to both aquatic life and human health. For instance, cyanide, which is highly effective in leaching gold from ore, can result in catastrophic spills that destroy aquatic habitats and poison drinking water supplies. The pollution of water bodies not only affects local communities but can also have far-reaching impacts on regional biodiversity. Fish populations, essential for the diets and economies of many communities, can suffer drastic declines, leading to food insecurity and loss of livelihood.

Energy Consumption and Carbon Footprint

Gold mining is an energy-intensive process, requiring significant amounts of electricity and fossil fuels for extraction, processing, and transportation. This high energy demand contributes to greenhouse gas emissions, exacerbating climate change. The carbon footprint associated with gold mining is substantial, particularly in regions where mining operations rely on coal or other non-renewable energy sources. As the world increasingly focuses on reducing carbon emissions and transitioning to greener energy models, the role of gold mining in this equation becomes a critical concern.

Waste Management Issues

The mining process generates vast quantities of waste materials, including tailings—finely ground rock that remains after the extraction of gold. These tailings often contain harmful substances and can be stored in tailings dams, which pose significant risks if they fail. The failure of tailings dams can lead to catastrophic events, releasing toxic materials into the environment and causing widespread damage to surrounding ecosystems and communities. Additionally, the management of waste materials is a complex issue, as improper disposal can lead to long-term contamination of soil and water sources.

Mitigation Efforts and Sustainable Practices

Recognizing the ecological footprint of gold mining, various stakeholders—including governments, NGOs, and mining companies—are beginning to adopt more sustainable practices. Efforts are being made to implement stricter environmental regulations, invest in cleaner technologies, and promote responsible mining initiatives. For example, some companies are exploring the use of less harmful chemicals in the extraction process and enhancing waste management practices to minimize environmental impacts.

Moreover, community-led initiatives that focus on sustainable mining practices are gaining traction. By involving local populations in decision-making processes and prioritizing environmental stewardship, these initiatives aim to balance economic benefits with ecological preservation.

Conclusion

The ecological footprint of gold mining is a complex interplay of environmental degradation, pollution, and social impact. As the demand for gold continues, it is imperative that the industry addresses these challenges through sustainable practices and responsible management. Only by acknowledging and mitigating the environmental consequences of gold mining can we ensure that the quest for this precious metal does not come at the expense of our planet's health and the well-being of its inhabitants.

Case Studies in Environmental Degradation

Gold mining has a long history of environmental degradation, with profound consequences for ecosystems and communities. This section explores several case studies that illustrate the various forms of harm caused by gold extraction processes, highlighting the need for more sustainable mining practices.

1. The Amazon Rainforest and Artisanal Mining

The Amazon rainforest, one of the most biodiverse regions on the planet, has suffered significantly from artisanal and small-scale gold mining (ASGM). In regions like Madre de Dios in Peru, illegal gold mining has led to extensive deforestation. Miners clear large swathes of forest to access gold deposits, resulting in habitat loss for countless species and the release of carbon stored in trees, exacerbating climate change. Additionally, mercury is frequently used in ASGM to separate gold from ore. This toxic metal contaminates local waterways and soil, posing severe health risks to nearby communities and wildlife. The cumulative impacts of deforestation, mercury pollution, and habitat destruction create a ripple effect, threatening the ecological balance of the rainforest.

2. The Ok Tedi Mine, Papua New Guinea

The Ok Tedi mine is one of the largest gold and copper mines in the world and has been the subject of significant environmental degradation since its inception in the 1980s. The mine discharges tailings directly into the Ok Tedi River, resulting in the contamination of water bodies and destruction of aquatic habitats. This practice has led to the siltation of rivers, disrupting fish populations and affecting the livelihoods of local communities dependent on fishing. Studies have reported a decline in fish catches and increased waterborne diseases among local populations, underscoring the health and economic impacts of environmental mismanagement.

3. The Yanacocha Mine, Peru

The Yanacocha mine, one of South America's largest gold mines, has faced criticism for its environmental practices. The mine's operations have led to the contamination of local water supplies with heavy metals and acids from mining activities. Residents in nearby communities have reported health issues linked to contaminated water, including skin diseases and gastrointestinal illnesses. Additionally, the mine's extensive land use for tailings and waste piles has resulted in significant landscape alteration, threatening local biodiversity. Protests from indigenous groups and environmental activists have highlighted the social and ecological consequences of gold mining in this region, leading to calls for more responsible mining practices.

4. The Goldfields of Western Australia
In Western Australia, the gold mining industry has caused substantial environmental degradation, particularly through land clearing and the use of cyanide in the extraction process. The use of cyanide, while effective in gold recovery, poses a risk of accidental spills, leading to contamination of soil and groundwater. Historical cases of cyanide spills have resulted in significant wildlife deaths, prompting concerns about the long-term impacts on local ecosystems. Moreover, land clearing for mining operations disrupts habitats and threatens endemic species, contributing to biodiversity loss in an already fragile environment.

5. The Marange Diamond Fields, Zimbabwe
While primarily known for diamonds, the Marange fields also have gold deposits that have attracted miners. The rapid influx of miners has led to severe environmental degradation, including deforestation, soil erosion, and water pollution. The unregulated nature of mining activities has caused significant ecological disruption, and the lack of environmental oversight has enabled practices that compromise the health of local ecosystems. Communities have reported increased incidences of waterborne diseases and loss of agricultural productivity due to soil degradation and contamination.

Conclusion
These case studies illustrate the complex interplay between gold mining and environmental degradation. The impacts of mining extend beyond immediate ecological harm, affecting the health and livelihoods of local communities. As the demand for gold continues, it is crucial to adopt sustainable practices that minimize environmental harm and promote the well-being of affected communities. Implementing stricter regulations, investing in eco-friendly technologies, and engaging local populations in decision-making processes are essential steps toward mitigating the negative environmental impacts of gold mining.

Efforts to Make Gold Mining Sustainable
The gold mining industry has long been associated with significant environmental degradation, including deforestation, soil erosion, water pollution, and biodiversity loss. As global awareness of environmental issues rises, there is a growing emphasis on sustainable mining practices that minimize the ecological footprint of gold extraction while still meeting the increasing demand for this precious metal. This section explores the various efforts being made within the industry to enhance sustainability in gold mining.

1. Adoption of Responsible Mining Practices
A fundamental shift towards responsible mining practices is underway, driven by both regulatory frameworks and corporate social responsibility (CSR) initiatives. Many mining

companies are adopting standards set by organizations such as the International Council on Mining and Metals (ICMM) and the World Gold Council's Responsible Gold Mining Principles. These frameworks emphasize transparency, ethical sourcing, and community engagement. Companies are increasingly required to assess and mitigate their environmental impacts throughout the mining lifecycle, from exploration and extraction to processing and closure.

2. Innovative Mining Technologies

Technological advancements are playing a critical role in enhancing the sustainability of gold mining. Innovations such as remote sensing, drones, and artificial intelligence are being utilized to improve exploration efficiency and reduce land disturbance. For instance, drones can monitor environmental changes and assess land use without extensive physical intrusion. Additionally, advances in mineral processing technology, such as the use of gravity separation and bioleaching, minimize the need for harmful chemicals, thereby reducing the risk of contamination to surrounding ecosystems.

3. Water Management Strategies

Water is a critical resource in gold mining, often leading to conflicts with local communities and ecosystems. Sustainable water management practices are being implemented to address these challenges. Mining operations are now focusing on water recycling and treatment systems that reduce the amount of freshwater required for processing ores. Closed-loop systems are designed to minimize water withdrawal from natural sources and prevent contamination. Moreover, some companies are investing in water stewardship initiatives that involve collaborating with local stakeholders to ensure equitable water access and protect surrounding watersheds.

4. Community Engagement and Development

Sustainable gold mining extends beyond environmental considerations to encompass social responsibility. Engaging with local communities is essential for fostering trust and ensuring that mining operations contribute positively to the areas in which they operate. Many mining companies are now prioritizing community development initiatives, including infrastructure improvements, education, and health care. By investing in local communities, the industry can help alleviate poverty, reduce social tensions, and create a more favorable operating environment.

5. Rehabilitation and Closure Planning

The end of a mine's productive life can pose significant environmental challenges if not managed properly. Sustainable mining practices involve comprehensive rehabilitation and closure planning that prioritizes restoring ecosystems and returning land to its natural state. Companies are increasingly required to develop closure plans before commencing operations, ensuring that environmental and social impacts are addressed long before a mine ceases production. Successful rehabilitation efforts can lead to the restoration of biodiversity and the creation of new land use opportunities, such as parks or agricultural land.

6. Certification and Traceability
Efforts to promote sustainable gold mining are supported by certification schemes that ensure gold is sourced responsibly. Initiatives such as the Fairmined and Fair Trade Gold certifications enable consumers to make informed choices by ensuring that the gold they purchase has been mined in a manner that respects both the environment and the rights of workers. Traceability systems are also being developed to track gold from its source to the final product, enhancing accountability and encouraging sustainable practices throughout the supply chain.

In conclusion, the gold mining industry is actively working to reduce its environmental impact through a combination of innovative technologies, responsible practices, and community engagement. While challenges remain, the ongoing efforts to implement sustainable mining practices are crucial for balancing economic benefits with environmental stewardship and social responsibility. As demand for gold continues, the industry's commitment to sustainability will play a vital role in shaping its future and preserving the planet for generations to come.

The Human Cost of Gold Mining: Health and Safety Concerns
Gold mining has long been associated with wealth and prosperity; however, the extraction process often comes at a severe human cost. The health and safety concerns for workers and communities involved in gold mining are profound and multifaceted, reflecting a complex interplay between economic necessity, environmental degradation, and human rights.

Health Risks for Workers
Gold mining can expose workers to a range of hazardous conditions, significantly impacting their health. One of the primary concerns is exposure to toxic chemicals, particularly mercury and cyanide, which are commonly used in the extraction process. Mercury, used in artisanal and small-scale mining (ASM) to amalgamate gold, poses severe risks, including neurological damage and respiratory issues. Workers often handle mercury without proper protective gear, leading to chronic exposure that can affect their health long after they leave the mines.

Moreover, the physical demands of mining work lead to a host of other health issues. The labor-intensive nature of mining can result in musculoskeletal disorders, chronic fatigue, and injuries from accidents. In many regions, especially where regulations are lax, miners work long hours in unsafe conditions, often without adequate safety training or equipment.

Environmental Impact and Community Health

The environmental consequences of gold mining extend beyond the immediate vicinity of the mines, affecting entire communities. The deforestation, soil degradation, and water contamination caused by mining operations can lead to significant public health issues. Contaminated water sources can carry heavy metals and other pollutants, leading to waterborne diseases and impacting local agriculture. Communities that rely on these water sources for drinking, cooking, and irrigation face heightened health risks, particularly among vulnerable populations such as children and the elderly.

Furthermore, mining activities can lead to increased rates of respiratory diseases due to dust and particulate matter released into the air. The proximity of mining operations to residential areas compounds these risks, as families live in close quarters with hazardous materials and activities.

Labor Rights and Exploitation

The socio-economic context of gold mining often places workers in precarious positions, vulnerable to exploitation and poor labor conditions. In many gold-mining regions, particularly in developing countries, labor rights may not be adequately protected. Workers frequently face low wages, lack of job security, and inadequate access to healthcare. These conditions are exacerbated by the informal nature of many mining operations, where workers have little recourse to advocate for their rights or improve their working conditions.

Child labor is another grim reality in some gold mining areas. Economic necessity drives families to involve their children in mining activities, which not only deprives them of education but also exposes them to the same health risks as adult workers. This cycle of poverty and exploitation further entrenches inequalities in the communities affected by gold mining.

Moving Towards Sustainable Practices

Recognizing these health and safety concerns, various organizations and governments are advocating for more sustainable mining practices. Initiatives aimed at reducing the use of toxic chemicals, enhancing safety standards, and promoting fair labor practices are crucial steps toward mitigating the human cost of gold mining. Community-led efforts to monitor mining activities and advocate for better working conditions also play a vital role in ensuring that the benefits of gold mining are equitably distributed.

In conclusion, while gold mining may contribute to economic development and wealth generation, it is imperative to address the health and safety concerns that accompany this industry. The impact on workers and communities must be prioritized, ensuring that the quest for gold does not come at the expense of human dignity and health. Sustainable practices, regulatory frameworks, and community engagement are essential to safeguard the well-being of those who toil in the shadow of this precious metal.

The Future of Ethical Gold: Certification and Standards

As the global demand for gold continues to rise, so too does the scrutiny surrounding its sourcing and production. The environmental, social, and ethical implications of gold mining have prompted a shift towards greater transparency and responsibility within the industry. Consumers are becoming increasingly aware of the ethical concerns associated with gold, leading to a demand for certified and responsibly sourced products. This section explores the future of ethical gold, focusing on certification and standards that empower consumers to make informed choices.

The Need for Ethical Gold

Gold has long been associated with wealth and beauty, but its extraction often comes at a significant cost to the environment and local communities. Traditional mining practices can lead to deforestation, water pollution, and the displacement of indigenous populations. Additionally, labor practices in some gold mines have raised concerns about human rights abuses, including child labor and exploitation. As awareness of these issues grows, consumers are increasingly seeking gold that is mined in a manner that respects both the planet and the people living in mining regions.

Certification Initiatives

In response to these concerns, a variety of certification initiatives and standards have emerged, aimed at promoting ethical practices in the gold supply chain. Among the most notable is the Responsible Jewellery Council (RJC), which provides a certification program for companies that adhere to ethical, social, and environmental standards. The RJC's Code of Practices outlines criteria that members must meet, including responsible sourcing, labor rights, and environmental stewardship.

Another important initiative is the Fairmined certification, which focuses on artisanal and small-scale mining. This certification ensures that gold is mined in a socially responsible and environmentally sustainable manner. Fairmined-certified gold supports fair wages for miners, community development projects, and the implementation of eco-friendly mining practices.

The Kimberley Process, while primarily aimed at preventing the trade in conflict diamonds, has also influenced the gold industry. By establishing a system of certification for gold sourced from conflict-affected areas, it has highlighted the importance of ensuring that gold is not financing violence or human rights abuses.

Consumer Awareness and Choice
As certification initiatives gain traction, consumer awareness is critical. Educating consumers about the importance of ethical gold and the various certification programs available empowers them to make informed purchasing decisions. Jewelers and retailers play a vital role in this process by providing information about the sourcing of their gold products and the certifications they adhere to.

The rise of online platforms and social media has further amplified the demand for transparency. Consumers can now easily access information about a brand's ethical practices, making it easier to choose responsibly sourced gold. As a result, brands that prioritize ethical sourcing are likely to gain a competitive advantage in the market.

The Role of Technology
Technological advancements are also shaping the future of ethical gold. Innovations in blockchain technology, for instance, offer the potential for enhanced traceability in the gold supply chain. By creating a tamper-proof record of a gold product's journey from mine to market, blockchain can provide consumers with verifiable information about its sourcing. This transparency fosters trust and encourages responsible practices among producers.

Looking Ahead
The future of ethical gold lies in the continued development of robust certification standards, increased consumer awareness, and the application of technology to enhance traceability. As the demand for ethically sourced gold grows, so too will the pressure on companies to adopt sustainable practices. By supporting certified gold, consumers can play an active role in promoting responsible mining practices that protect the environment and uphold human rights. This shift not only benefits communities involved in gold production but also contributes to a more sustainable future for the industry as a whole.

In conclusion, the path toward ethical gold is paved with opportunities for collaboration, innovation, and consumer choice. As we move forward, the collective efforts of consumers, brands, and certification bodies will shape a gold market that values integrity, responsibility, and sustainability.

Chapter 11

The Economics of Gold

The Price of Gold: Historical Trends

The price of gold has been one of the most dynamic and closely monitored economic indicators throughout history. Its value has fluctuated widely due to various factors, including economic conditions, geopolitical events, and shifts in investor sentiment. Understanding these historical trends provides insight into gold's role as a commodity, a currency, and a store of value.

Ancient and Medieval Periods

In ancient civilizations, gold was primarily valued for its rarity and beauty, serving as a medium of exchange and a symbol of wealth. The earliest known uses of gold can be traced back to around 3000 BCE in Egypt, where it was used to create jewelry and artifacts for the elite. During these times, gold's value was not measured in a standardized way; instead, it was determined by its intrinsic qualities and the social and political contexts in which it was used.

As societies evolved, particularly in the medieval period, gold began to take on more standardized forms of valuation. The introduction of coinage in the 7th century BCE marked a significant shift; gold coins became a key component of trade. The price of gold began to reflect its minting costs, the availability of gold deposits, and the political stability of the regions producing it. In medieval Europe, the value of gold was often tied to the fluctuating economies and the political landscape, especially during times of war or economic instability.

The Gold Standard Era

The 19th century saw the establishment of the gold standard, a monetary system where the value of a country's currency was directly linked to a specific amount of gold. This period marked a significant stabilization in the price of gold, as it became recognized globally as a reliable measure of currency value. For example, the Gold Rushes in the mid-1800s, particularly in California and Australia, led to an influx of gold that temporarily decreased its price, as supply outpaced demand.

However, the gold standard system also meant that the price of gold was relatively stable, with governments controlling its valuation through monetary policy. The standard was abandoned during World War I as nations suspended gold convertibility to finance the war, leading to significant fluctuations in gold prices.

Post-Gold Standard Developments

The end of the Bretton Woods Agreement in 1971 marked a pivotal moment in gold pricing. The U.S. dollar was no longer convertible into gold, leading to a free-floating gold market. This transition resulted in a dramatic increase in gold prices, which surged from around $35 per ounce in the early 1970s to over $800 by 1980, driven by inflation, economic uncertainty, and rising geopolitical tensions, including the Cold War.

In the following decades, gold prices experienced volatility due to various factors such as economic recessions, changes in monetary policy, and shifts in investor sentiment. The late 1990s and early 2000s saw a gradual increase in gold prices as central banks began to diversify their reserves, leading to increased demand in the market.

The 21st Century and Recent Trends

Entering the 21st century, gold prices reached new heights, peaking at over $1,900 per ounce in September 2011 amid concerns over the global financial crisis and inflation. The resurgence of gold as a "safe haven" asset during economic downturns has contributed to its rising prices. Factors such as fluctuating currency values, trade tensions, and geopolitical conflicts continue to influence gold's market price today.

In recent years, the price of gold has undergone significant fluctuations, influenced by global economic conditions, the COVID-19 pandemic, and shifts toward digital currencies. As central banks increase their gold reserves and investors turn to gold during crises, its historical trends suggest that it will remain a vital component of the global economy and a barometer of financial stability.

In conclusion, the price of gold has transformed dramatically over millennia, reflecting humanity's evolving relationship with this precious metal. From ancient currency to modern-day investment, gold's enduring value is anchored in its rarity, cultural significance, and the economic realities of the times.

Gold as an Investment: Safe Haven or Risky Bet?

Gold has long been regarded as a valuable asset, often viewed as a safe haven during times of economic uncertainty. Its unique properties and historical significance contribute to its appeal as an investment. However, like any asset class, investing in gold comes with both advantages and disadvantages that potential investors should carefully consider.

Pros of Investing in Gold

1. Hedge Against Inflation: One of the primary reasons investors flock to gold is its ability to act as a hedge against inflation. When inflation rises, the purchasing power of fiat currencies tends to decrease, leading investors to seek stability in tangible assets like gold. Historically, gold prices have tended to rise when inflationary pressures increase, providing a safeguard for wealth.

2. Crisis Commodity: Gold is often termed a "crisis commodity" due to its historical performance during geopolitical turmoil and economic crises. During periods of financial instability, such as the 2008 financial crisis or the COVID-19 pandemic, gold prices surged as investors sought refuge from volatile markets. This characteristic makes gold an appealing option for diversification in uncertain times.

3. Diversification: Including gold in an investment portfolio can help reduce overall risk. Gold typically has a low or negative correlation with other asset classes like stocks and bonds, meaning it may not move in tandem with these investments. This diversification can smooth out returns and mitigate losses during market downturns.

4. Intrinsic Value: Unlike paper currencies, which can be printed in unlimited quantities, gold has a finite supply. Its intrinsic value stems from its physical properties, rarity, and historical significance. This quality lends gold a sense of durability and reliability, especially in times of economic distress.

5. Global Acceptance: Gold is recognized and valued worldwide, making it a universally accepted form of wealth. Investors can liquidate gold relatively easily in most markets, providing flexibility and accessibility when needed.

Cons of Investing in Gold

1. Price Volatility: While gold is often seen as a safe haven, its price can be highly volatile in the short term. Factors such as changes in interest rates, currency fluctuations, and shifts in investor sentiment can lead to significant price swings. This volatility can pose risks for investors looking for stable returns.

2. No Dividends or Interest: Unlike stocks or bonds, gold does not generate income through dividends or interest. Investors in gold rely solely on price appreciation for returns, which can be a drawback in a low-growth environment. This lack of cash flow can make gold less attractive compared to other investments that provide regular income.

3. Storage and Insurance Costs: Physical gold requires secure storage, which can incur additional costs. Investors must consider the expenses associated with safekeeping gold, including insurance and storage fees. For those investing in gold bullion or coins, these costs can erode potential profits.

4. Market Sentiment Dependency: Gold prices can be heavily influenced by market sentiment, which can lead to speculative bubbles. Investor psychology plays a significant role in the demand for gold, and sudden shifts in sentiment can result in rapid price declines. This dependency on market mood makes gold a risky investment for some.

5. Long-Term Performance: Although gold has performed well in certain periods, its long-term growth potential may not match that of equities. Over decades, equities have historically outperformed gold in terms of returns, making gold a less appealing choice for long-term investors seeking substantial growth.

Conclusion
Investing in gold can be a double-edged sword. It offers unique benefits as a hedge against inflation, a crisis commodity, and a means of diversification. However, potential investors must weigh these advantages against the risks of price volatility, lack of income generation, and associated storage costs. Ultimately, whether gold is a safe haven or a risky bet depends on individual investment goals, market conditions, and personal financial situations. As with any investment, thorough research and a clear understanding of one's risk tolerance are essential for making informed decisions.

The Role of Gold in Inflation and Deflation
Gold has long been regarded as a hedge against inflation and a store of value, a sentiment that has persisted through centuries of economic fluctuation. Understanding how gold prices interact with economic conditions, particularly inflation and deflation, is essential for grasping its role in both historical and modern economies.

Gold as an Inflation Hedge
Inflation, characterized by a general rise in prices and a decrease in purchasing power, often leads investors to seek refuge in tangible assets that can retain value. Gold historically fits this description, as its intrinsic worth does not diminish with the devaluation of currency. When inflation rises, the real returns on cash and fixed-income investments tend to decline, prompting

investors to allocate resources toward gold. This behavior drives up demand, which in turn elevates gold prices.

The correlation between gold and inflation can be observed in various economic contexts. For instance, during the 1970s, the U.S. experienced significant inflation, with rates peaking in the double digits. During this period, gold prices surged from approximately $35 an ounce in 1970 to over $800 by 1980, as investors increasingly turned to gold as a safe haven. This transition reflects a broader trend: as inflation expectations rise, so too does the appeal of gold as a protective asset.

Gold in Deflationary Periods

Conversely, during deflationary periods—where prices decline, and economic activity slows—gold's role becomes more complex. In these instances, the purchasing power of currency increases, making it less critical for investors to seek gold as a safeguard. Deflation often leads to a decrease in gold prices as demand wanes. Notably, the Great Depression of the 1930s serves as a historical example; despite the economic turmoil, gold prices remained relatively stable compared to the dramatic deflation of the U.S. dollar.

However, while gold may not perform as strongly during deflationary times, it can still maintain a level of appeal for investors seeking to diversify their portfolios. In situations where central banks may respond to deflation by implementing quantitative easing or lowering interest rates, the potential for inflation to follow can lead investors back to gold as a precautionary measure.

The Dual Role of Gold in Economic Conditions

The interaction of gold prices with inflation and deflation underscores its dual nature as both a reactive and proactive investment. In inflationary environments, gold serves almost as a reflexive asset—its prices rise as a natural response to increasing demand driven by fears of currency devaluation. In contrast, during deflationary spells, while it may not be the primary focus, gold remains a viable asset for those looking to hedge against potential future inflation or economic instability.

The psychological aspect also plays a significant role in these dynamics. Investor sentiment, driven by perceptions of economic outlook and stability, heavily influences gold prices. The fear of inflation or the consequences of central bank policies can spark movements in gold investment, reflecting broader economic sentiments.

Conclusion

In summary, the role of gold in inflation and deflation is marked by its historical significance and emotional resonance in the financial markets. As a hedge against inflation, gold retains its allure during periods of rising prices, while its performance during deflationary times hinges on investor sentiment and broader economic policy responses. Whether as a response to current economic conditions or as a protective measure against future uncertainties, gold remains a critical component of investment strategies in an ever-evolving economic landscape. As both inflationary and deflationary pressures continue to shape financial markets, gold's timeless appeal as a store of value is likely to endure.

Gold and Currency Fluctuations

Gold has long been revered not just as a precious metal but also as a universal store of value, making it integral to the relationship between gold prices and currency values. This relationship is influenced by a multitude of factors, including economic conditions, inflation rates, interest rates, and geopolitical stability.

At its core, the price of gold is often inversely related to the strength of major currencies, particularly the U.S. dollar. When the dollar weakens, gold prices tend to rise, making it a hedge against currency devaluation. Conversely, when the dollar strengthens, gold prices often decline. This phenomenon occurs because gold is typically priced in U.S. dollars. Therefore, when the dollar loses value, it takes more dollars to purchase the same amount of gold, driving up its price.

One of the most critical factors that affect gold prices is inflation. Historically, gold has been viewed as a safeguard against inflation. When inflation rises, the purchasing power of currency declines, prompting investors to flock to gold as a tangible asset that retains value over time. For instance, during periods of high inflation, such as the 1970s in the United States, gold prices soared as investors sought refuge from eroding currency value. In contrast, during deflationary periods, gold prices may stagnate as confidence in currency increases.

Interest rates also play a significant role in determining gold prices. Higher interest rates typically lead to a stronger currency, as they attract foreign capital looking for better returns on investments. When interest rates rise, the opportunity cost of holding non-yielding assets like gold increases, leading to a reduction in gold demand and subsequently a decrease in its price. Conversely, when interest rates are low or are projected to fall, the allure of gold increases, as the cost of holding it becomes less burdensome, driving prices higher.

Geopolitical factors can also induce volatility in both currency values and gold prices. During times of uncertainty—such as wars, political unrest, or economic crises—investors often turn to gold as a "safe haven" asset. For instance, during the 2008 financial crisis, as confidence in the global financial system waned, gold prices surged dramatically as investors sought stability outside of traditional financial markets. Similarly, currency fluctuations resulting from geopolitical tensions can lead to increased gold prices as investors hedge against perceived risks.

Additionally, the relationship between gold and currencies is often depicted through the Gold-to-Silver Ratio and other precious metal ratios, which can provide insight into market dynamics. Traders and investors frequently analyze these ratios to gauge market sentiment and make informed decisions.

It is important to note that while gold traditionally serves as a hedge against currency fluctuations, it is not immune to market forces. Speculation, mining production levels, and changes in central bank policies can also influence gold prices. Central banks, in particular, have a unique role in this dynamic. When central banks buy or sell gold, they can significantly impact its price, as these transactions can alter the supply and demand balance.

In summary, the relationship between gold prices and currency values is complex and multifaceted, shaped by economic indicators, investor behavior, and geopolitical events. As a timeless asset, gold continues to be a critical component in the global financial landscape, offering both a barometer for economic health and a refuge in times of uncertainty. Understanding this relationship is essential for investors, policymakers, and anyone interested in the dynamics of global finance.

The Future of Gold in Global Finance

As we navigate the complexities of the 21st century, gold remains a pivotal asset in global finance, with its role evolving alongside technological advancements, geopolitical tensions, and economic fluctuations. Historically viewed as a safe haven during periods of economic turmoil, gold's significance is being re-examined in light of emerging financial paradigms, including cryptocurrency, digital currencies, and shifts in monetary policy.

Gold as a Safe Haven Asset

Gold has long been regarded as a hedge against inflation and currency devaluation. In uncertain economic climates, investors often flock to gold, driving up its value. This trend is likely to persist as economic instability due to factors like geopolitical tensions, pandemics, and climate change continues to affect global markets. Central banks, particularly in emerging economies, are increasingly diversifying their reserves by accumulating gold to mitigate risks related to fiat currency fluctuations. In recent years, countries like Russia and China have significantly increased their gold reserves, indicating a strategic shift towards this precious metal as a means of bolstering financial security.

Integration with Digital Finance

The rise of digital currencies and blockchain technology has introduced new dimensions to the financial landscape. While some view cryptocurrencies like Bitcoin as a modern substitute for gold, others argue that they complement rather than replace it. The intrinsic value of gold, derived from its scarcity, physical properties, and historical significance as a store of value, remains unmatched by digital assets. However, gold is also making its way into the digital realm, with the development of gold-backed cryptocurrencies that combine the stability of gold with the efficiency of blockchain technology. This hybrid model could attract a new generation of investors seeking the security of gold while engaging in the fast-paced world of digital finance.

The Role of Gold in Monetary Policy

Central banks' monetary policies are continuously adapting to the changing economic environment. While the gold standard is no longer a prevalent system, the notion of backing currencies with gold is gaining traction among some economists and policymakers who advocate for a return to a more stable monetary framework. This could be particularly relevant in times of hyperinflation or extreme economic distress, where confidence in fiat currencies wanes. As discussions around monetary reform gain momentum, gold may once again find itself at the center of financial discourse.

Sustainable Investing and Ethical Gold

Amid growing concerns about environmental sustainability and ethical practices, the future of gold in global finance will also be influenced by the demand for responsibly sourced gold. Investors are increasingly prioritizing Environmental, Social, and Governance (ESG) criteria when making investment decisions. The gold industry is responding with initiatives aimed at promoting sustainable mining practices, reducing environmental impact, and ensuring fair labor conditions. These efforts are likely to enhance gold's appeal as a socially responsible investment, further integrating it into the modern financial ecosystem.

Challenges Ahead

Despite its enduring allure, gold faces challenges that could affect its future role in global finance. The volatility of global markets, technological disruptions, and evolving investor preferences may alter the dynamics of gold investment. Additionally, the continuing development of central bank digital currencies (CBDCs) poses potential competition for gold as a store of value. As governments explore the implementation of CBDCs, the relationship between traditional assets like gold and emerging digital currencies will require careful monitoring.

In conclusion, the future of gold in global finance appears to be one of adaptation and integration. Its historical status as a safe haven asset, combined with the burgeoning digital economy and a growing emphasis on sustainability, positions gold to maintain its relevance in an ever-evolving financial landscape. As the world continues to confront economic uncertainty and technological advancements, gold's enduring legacy as a symbol of wealth and stability will likely ensure its continued role in shaping the future of finance.

Chapter 12

Gold and Society

Gold and Social Stratification

Gold has long been a symbol of wealth, power, and status across civilizations, serving as an intrinsic marker of social stratification. The allure of this precious metal has not only shaped individual fortunes but also influenced societal structures throughout history. From ancient civilizations to modern economies, gold has played a pivotal role in defining social hierarchies, wealth distribution, and cultural identities.

In ancient societies, gold was often associated with divinity and royalty. For instance, in Ancient Egypt, gold was considered the flesh of the gods, and pharaohs adorned themselves with gold jewelry and artifacts to signify their divine right to rule. The lavish burial practices of pharaohs, including the famous tomb of Tutankhamun, exemplified the connection between gold and power. These practices reinforced social stratification, as only the elite could afford such opulent displays, while the lower classes remained in poverty. In this context, gold not only represented wealth but also served as a tangible representation of authority and spiritual significance.

Similarly, in Mesopotamia—often viewed as the cradle of civilization—gold was central to the economic and social fabric. The emergence of trade and commerce saw gold coins introduced as currency, facilitating exchanges and establishing a wealth-based economy. Those who controlled gold resources, such as the ruling class and merchant elites, wielded significant influence over societal norms and practices. This created a distinct divide between the wealthy and the impoverished, shaping the political landscape of the time.

As societies evolved, the association between gold and social stratification persisted. In Ancient Rome, gold became emblematic of status and power. The elite class, known as the patricians, amassed vast fortunes through agriculture, trade, and military conquests. Gold jewelry, elaborate home decor, and opulent feasts became markers of wealth, reinforcing social divisions. The phrase "golden" often described not just the material itself but also the elevated social standing that accompanied it. The influx of gold from conquests further exacerbated these divisions, as wealth concentrated in the hands of a few while the majority labored for their survival.

The Middle Ages witnessed a continuation of this trend, as gold became synonymous with nobility and feudal power. Monarchs and landowners used gold to assert their dominance and influence over their subjects. The goldsmiths of the time, who crafted intricate jewelry and religious artifacts, were also seen as elevated figures within society. However, the reliance on gold often led to stark contrasts in social mobility, as the lower classes remained marginalized and disenfranchised.

With the advent of the Age of Exploration, the quest for gold spurred imperial ambitions and colonial expansion, leading to profound social disparities. European powers sought to extract gold from the New World, which had devastating consequences for indigenous populations. Gold mining operations often relied on forced labor, reinforcing a system of exploitation that further entrenched social hierarchies based on wealth and power.

In modern times, while the direct association between gold and social class may have shifted, its legacy endures. Gold remains a critical asset in global finance and personal wealth accumulation. The disparity in access to gold and its derivatives continues to reflect and reinforce existing social inequalities. The wealthy often use gold as a hedge against economic uncertainties, whereas marginalized communities may struggle to access even basic necessities.

In conclusion, the historical association of gold with social stratification highlights the complex interplay between wealth, power, and identity. Gold has served not only as a medium of exchange but also as a symbol of status, shaping societal structures throughout human history. Understanding this relationship offers valuable insights into the ongoing dynamics of wealth distribution and social class in contemporary society, where gold's allure continues to captivate and divide.

The Role of Gold in Symbolizing Wealth

Gold has long held a prominent position in the human psyche as a symbol of wealth, success, and power. Its unique properties—such as its lustrous appearance, malleability, and resistance to tarnish—have contributed to its desirability throughout history. This allure can be traced back to ancient civilizations, where gold was not merely a metal but a representation of divine favor and social status.

Historical Context

From the time of ancient Egypt, where gold was associated with the sun god Ra and used extensively in burial artifacts to ensure a prosperous afterlife, the metal's connection to wealth and power became firmly established. Egyptian pharaohs adorned themselves with gold jewelry and decorated their tombs with gold artifacts, reinforcing the notion that gold was integral to both earthly power and spiritual significance. Similarly, in Mesopotamia, gold played a vital role in trade and commerce, symbolizing wealth that could elevate an individual's social standing.

As societies evolved, so too did the role of gold in signaling prosperity. In the classical world, the Greeks and Romans utilized gold not only in currency but also in art and architecture, often linking it to their gods and the ideals of beauty and excellence. The use of gold coins standardized wealth across empires, allowing for trade and commerce to flourish, and thus embedding gold deeper into the fabric of economic life.

Cultural Significance

Gold's status as a symbol of wealth transcends geographical boundaries and historical periods. In many cultures, it is associated with beauty, purity, and the divine. For instance, in Chinese culture, gold is often linked with prosperity and good fortune, making it a popular choice for gifts during important celebrations such as weddings and the Lunar New Year. This cultural significance is further reflected in the traditional practice of gifting gold jewelry, which is seen as a means of securing financial stability and social status.

In Western societies, the representation of gold as a status symbol has persisted into modern times. The phrase "the golden age" evokes images of prosperity and success, while gold remains a central element in awards such as the Academy Awards, where the coveted Oscar statue is made of gold-plated bronze. This continuous association reinforces the idea that gold is not merely a physical commodity but an emblem of achievement.

Economic Implications

The economic significance of gold as a symbol of wealth is also noteworthy. Historically, gold served as the foundation for monetary systems, leading to the establishment of the gold standard in the 19th century. This system linked currency values to gold reserves, effectively making gold synonymous with financial security and stability. Even after the abandonment of the gold standard, gold continues to be viewed as a safe haven during economic uncertainty, often experiencing price surges in times of inflation or market volatility.

Contemporary Perspectives

Today, gold remains a quintessential marker of wealth. From luxury jewelry to gold bars and coins, it is seen as a tangible asset that retains value over time. The desire for gold is ingrained in various aspects of society, including finance, fashion, and art. In investment circles, gold is often referred to as a "safe haven" asset, a testament to its lasting allure and status as a reliable store of value.

Conclusion

In conclusion, gold's role as a symbol of wealth is deeply rooted in historical, cultural, and economic contexts. Its unique properties and historical significance have cemented its status as the ultimate representation of success and prosperity. As societies evolve, the allure of gold continues to captivate, proving that its symbolism transcends time, remaining an enduring testament to humanity's complex relationship with wealth and power.

Gold and Poverty: The Paradoxes of Wealth

Gold has long been a symbol of wealth and prosperity, yet its mining can create profound inequalities, leading to a paradox that enriches some while impoverishing others. This duality is particularly evident in regions where gold mining is prevalent, often transforming local economies, social structures, and the environment in complex ways.

Economic Enrichment and Employment Opportunities

In many gold-rich regions, mining can provide significant economic benefits. The influx of investment and the establishment of mining operations can generate jobs for local communities, offering employment opportunities that might not otherwise exist. For instance, gold mines often employ thousands of workers, leading to an increase in income for families and stimulating local businesses. This economic activity can catalyze infrastructure development, such as roads, schools, and hospitals, further benefiting the community.

Moreover, the taxes and royalties generated from gold mining can contribute to national revenues, which, in theory, should fund public services and development projects. Countries rich in gold, such as Ghana and Mali, have seen varying degrees of economic growth attributed to gold production.

The Shadow of Exploitation and Inequality

However, the benefits of gold mining are frequently accompanied by exploitation and inequality. Large multinational corporations often dominate the gold mining industry, leading to a concentration of wealth that rarely trickles down to local communities. While mining companies may promise employment and development, the reality can be starkly different. Many workers are employed under precarious and exploitative conditions, facing long hours, low wages, and inadequate safety measures. Reports of child labor and human rights abuses in artisanal and small-scale mining operations further underscore the darker side of gold extraction.

In regions where gold mining has thrived, the wealth generated often exacerbates existing inequalities. Those with power and resources—typically the mining companies and local elites—reap the majority of the economic benefits, while local populations are left with environmental degradation and social disruption. This disparity can create tensions within communities, leading to conflicts over land rights, resource control, and access to mining revenues.

Environmental Degradation and Health Risks

The environmental impact of gold mining can also contribute to poverty. Mining operations often lead to deforestation, water pollution, and soil degradation, severely affecting agricultural productivity and the health of local ecosystems. Communities dependent on agriculture or fishing may find their livelihoods compromised, forcing them into deeper poverty. The health risks associated with mining, including exposure to toxic chemicals such as mercury and cyanide, further threaten the well-being of local populations, leading to increased medical costs and lost productivity.

The Cycle of Poverty and Dependency

The paradox of wealth created by gold mining can trap communities in a cycle of poverty and dependency. When mining companies extract resources and leave without fulfilling their promises, local economies can suffer long-term consequences. The boom-and-bust cycle of gold prices can also lead to economic instability, where communities reliant on mining face sudden downturns when gold prices fall. This volatility can drive families into poverty, undermining any initial benefits that mining may have provided.

A Path Forward: Sustainable Practices and Community Empowerment

Addressing the paradox of wealth associated with gold mining requires a commitment to sustainable practices and community empowerment. Governments, corporations, and local communities must work together to ensure that the benefits of gold mining are equitably distributed. This includes implementing fair labor practices, investing in local infrastructure, and establishing transparent systems for revenue sharing.

Moreover, efforts to promote artisanal and small-scale mining can help local communities take control of their resources, provided that these practices are regulated to minimize environmental impact and ensure workers' rights. By fostering a more inclusive and sustainable approach to gold mining, it is possible to mitigate the paradox of wealth, allowing communities to thrive rather than suffer under the weight of their natural resources.

In conclusion, while gold mining can be a source of wealth, it is crucial to recognize and address the accompanying challenges of poverty, exploitation, and environmental degradation to create a more equitable future for affected communities.

The Ethics of Gold Ownership: Hoarding vs. Sharing

Gold has long been a symbol of wealth, power, and status in human society, and its allure has not diminished over the centuries. From ancient civilizations that adorned their temples with gold to modern investors who hoard it as a safe haven asset, the ownership of gold raises complex ethical questions. At the heart of this discourse is the dichotomy between hoarding and sharing, which prompts an examination of moral implications surrounding gold accumulation in contemporary society.

Hoarding Gold: A Reflection of Individualism and Security
The act of hoarding gold can be seen as an expression of individualism and self-preservation. In unstable economic climates, individuals often turn to gold as a tangible asset that can safeguard their wealth against inflation, currency devaluation, and financial crises. The intrinsic value of gold, coupled with its historical role as a universal currency, makes it a desirable asset for safeguarding personal wealth. This instinct to accumulate gold can be viewed as a rational response to economic uncertainty, driven by a desire for security and stability.

However, the ethical implications of hoarding gold become more pronounced when considering social responsibility. The concentration of gold in the hands of a few contributes to wealth inequality, a phenomenon that can perpetuate social stratification. When significant amounts of gold are held by individuals or corporations, it can detract from the collective wealth of communities and nations, limiting access to resources and opportunities for those less fortunate. This hoarding behavior raises questions about moral obligations: Should individuals prioritize their own security over the welfare of others?

The Case for Sharing Gold: Collective Welfare and Responsibility
On the opposite end of the spectrum lies the concept of sharing gold, which embodies principles of social responsibility, altruism, and community welfare. Sharing gold—whether through charitable donations, community investments, or even cooperative gold ownership—can have profound positive impacts on society. For example, wealth generated from gold mining can be invested in local communities to improve education, healthcare, and infrastructure. This approach can help bridge the gap between the wealthy and the impoverished, creating a more equitable society.

Sharing gold can also inspire collective action during economic downturns. Community-led initiatives can mobilize resources to support vulnerable populations, demonstrating that wealth does not solely exist for individual gain but can be a tool for empowerment and upliftment. Furthermore, in cultures that value communal living, the act of sharing wealth, including gold, aligns with ethical norms that prioritize collective well-being over individual accumulation.

The Moral Dilemma: Balancing Personal Gain with Social Impact
The ethics of gold ownership thus presents a moral dilemma: how to balance the personal desire for wealth with the implications of that accumulation for society at large. Individuals must confront the question of whether their ownership of gold serves merely as a vehicle for personal enrichment or if it can be leveraged for broader social good.

In exploring this ethical landscape, it becomes essential to consider alternative frameworks for gold ownership. Practicing responsible stewardship of gold—through ethical mining practices, support for fair trade, and transparency in ownership—can help mitigate some of the negative implications of hoarding. Additionally, creating systems that encourage shared ownership models or community investments can foster a culture of collaboration rather than competition.

Conclusion: A Path Forward
Ultimately, the ethical considerations surrounding gold ownership call for a deeper reflection on values, priorities, and responsibilities. As gold continues to captivate human imagination and remains a significant economic asset, individuals and societies must navigate the complex interplay between hoarding and sharing. Embracing a more ethical approach to gold ownership can lead to a more equitable distribution of wealth, fostering a society where prosperity is not just a privilege for the few but a shared responsibility. In this way, gold can transcend its role as a mere symbol of wealth and instead become a catalyst for positive change.

Gold and Global Inequality: Bridging the Gap
Gold has long been a symbol of wealth, status, and power, but its distribution and the access to its wealth have created significant disparities both within and between nations. The global gold market is characterized by complexities that intertwine economic policies, local practices, and broader geopolitical dynamics, which collectively shape how gold wealth is allocated and who benefits from it.

The Concentration of Gold Wealth
Historically, gold has been a major driver of wealth accumulation for certain nations and elite individuals. Countries rich in gold reserves, such as South Africa, Australia, and Russia, have leveraged these resources to enhance their economic standing. However, the wealth generated from gold mining in these regions often fails to benefit local communities. Large mining corporations frequently extract gold with little regard for the environmental and social repercussions, leading to wealth concentration among a few stakeholders while communities face issues such as displacement, health hazards, and environmental degradation.

In many gold-rich countries, the economic benefits of gold mining are not equitably distributed. For instance, in countries like Ghana and Mali, where gold mining represents a significant portion of national GDP, the local populations frequently remain impoverished. Corruption, poor governance, and a lack of effective regulatory frameworks contribute to this inequitable distribution. The wealth generated from gold extraction often flows out of the local economies, enriching multinational corporations and foreign investors while leaving local communities struggling for basic resources.

The Role of Artisanal and Small-Scale Mining
Contrasting with industrial mining, artisanal and small-scale gold mining (ASGM) presents a complex picture in the context of global inequality. While ASGM can provide livelihoods for millions of people in developing countries, it often operates in a legal gray area. Workers in this

sector typically face harsh working conditions, lack access to proper safety measures, and receive minimal financial compensation for their labor. Despite these challenges, ASGM contributes significantly to local economies, enabling communities to access gold wealth directly.

However, the informal nature of ASGM also perpetuates inequality. Without legal recognition, miners are vulnerable to exploitation and may not receive fair prices for their gold. This situation exacerbates existing inequalities, as wealth generated through ASGM is often subject to local and international market fluctuations that do not favor the miners.

International Trade and Economic Policies

The international gold trade further complicates the picture of global inequality. Gold is treated as a commodity on global markets, subject to speculative trading practices that can lead to price volatility. Countries that rely heavily on gold exports can find themselves at the mercy of global price fluctuations, which can destabilize their economies and exacerbate poverty. For example, during periods of low gold prices, countries like Zimbabwe and Ghana have experienced severe economic downturns, impacting not only the mining sector but also broader economic stability.

The concept of "resource curse" highlights how countries rich in natural resources, including gold, often experience slower economic growth and poorer development outcomes compared to those with fewer natural resources. This paradox is attributed to various factors, including political instability, corruption, and conflict over resource control, which can hinder equitable development.

Bridging the Gap

Addressing the inequalities associated with gold wealth requires a multifaceted approach. Governments, civil society, and international organizations must collaborate to implement policies that promote fair trade practices, ensure equitable distribution of resources, and provide legal protections for artisanal miners. Initiatives aimed at improving transparency in gold supply chains, such as the OECD Due Diligence Guidance for Responsible Supply Chains, can also play a pivotal role in bridging the gap.

Moreover, investing in community-led initiatives can empower local populations to benefit directly from gold mining activities. Education, infrastructure development, and access to financial resources can help transform gold wealth into sustainable economic growth, reducing disparities and fostering more equitable societies.

In conclusion, while gold has the potential to drive economic development and prosperity, its distribution often reflects and reinforces global inequalities. Bridging this gap requires concerted efforts from various stakeholders to ensure that gold wealth benefits all, rather than a privileged few.

Chapter 13

Gold in Modern Culture

Gold in Fashion

Gold has long been synonymous with wealth, power, and prestige, and its influence permeates the world of fashion in ways that are both profound and multifaceted. This precious metal has transcended its utilitarian roots, evolving into a potent symbol of status and luxury that continues to captivate designers, consumers, and cultural icons alike.

Historically, gold has been woven into the narrative of fashion since ancient civilizations. In Egypt, for instance, pharaohs adorned themselves with intricate gold jewelry not just for adornment but as a means of demonstrating their divine authority and opulence. Gold's lustrous quality made it a preferred choice for crafting exquisite pieces that signified wealth and power. As time progressed, this tradition persisted, with gold often featuring prominently in the wardrobes of aristocrats and royalty across Europe and Asia, further cementing its status as a symbol of luxury.

In contemporary fashion, gold maintains its allure, appearing in various forms across the spectrum of clothing and accessories. From haute couture collections to everyday streetwear, designers have embraced gold, utilizing it in fabrics, embellishments, and jewelry. The incorporation of gold into garments—such as shimmering gold-threaded fabrics or metallic finishes—adds a touch of extravagance and glamour. Notable designers like Chanel, Versace, and Dolce & Gabbana have often featured gold in their collections, reinforcing its status as a marker of high fashion.

Jewelry, however, stands as the most direct representation of gold's role in fashion. Gold jewelry is often seen as a definitive statement of style and social standing. Whether it's a simple gold chain, an ornate bracelet, or a statement ring, the choice to wear gold communicates a message of affluence and taste. In many cultures, gold jewelry is also associated with significant life events—wedding bands, family heirlooms, and celebratory gifts—further intertwining the metal with personal and cultural identity.

Moreover, gold has found its place in the realm of celebrity culture, where it serves as a tool for self-expression and brand identity. High-profile events such as the Oscars and Met Gala often showcase celebrities donning extravagant gold ensembles and jewelry, turning red carpets into showcases of opulence. The visibility of gold in these contexts amplifies its status as a fashion icon, influencing trends and consumer behavior.

The psychological appeal of gold in fashion cannot be overlooked. The color gold is often associated with warmth, richness, and vibrancy, evoking feelings of exuberance and luxury. This psychological connection enhances the desirability of gold items, as consumers seek to embody the qualities that gold represents. Furthermore, the rarity of gold contributes to its allure; as a finite resource, its scarcity elevates its status in the eyes of consumers, making gold items not just fashion statements but investments in personal wealth.

In recent years, the fashion industry has also begun to embrace sustainability, leading to a resurgence in recycled gold jewelry and ethical fashion practices. Consumers are increasingly aware of the environmental and ethical implications of their purchases, prompting designers to source gold responsibly. This evolution reflects a growing awareness of the need for a balance between luxury and sustainability while maintaining gold's status as a symbol of prestige.

In conclusion, gold's enduring presence in fashion as the ultimate status symbol is a testament to its historical significance and cultural impact. As it continues to evolve within the realms of design, celebrity influence, and ethical considerations, gold remains a captivating marker of style, wealth, and personal expression, solidifying its place at the forefront of fashion for generations to come.

Gold in Music and Entertainment: From Bling to Lyrics

Gold has long been a symbol of wealth, power, and status, deeply embedded in human culture and society. In modern music and entertainment, gold continues to captivate audiences, serving both as a literal and metaphorical reference. Its representation spans genres and styles, from hip-hop culture to pop anthems, often reflecting societal values, aspirations, and the complexities of human identity.

In the realm of hip-hop, gold jewelry—often referred to as "bling"—has become a powerful symbol of success and affluence. Artists like Jay-Z, Kanye West, and Nicki Minaj prominently showcase gold chains, rings, and watches, which serve not only as fashion statements but also as markers of their journey from humble beginnings to celebrity status. This ostentation is not merely for aesthetic appeal; it expresses a narrative of triumph over adversity, encapsulating the aspirational ethos that characterizes much of the genre. The bling culture in hip-hop often critiques materialism while simultaneously celebrating it, creating a paradox that resonates with listeners.

Beyond fashion, gold frequently appears in song lyrics as a metaphor for value and desirability. Tracks like "Gold Digger" by Kanye West explore themes of wealth and relationships, intertwining the allure of gold with social commentary on materialism and dependency. Similarly, in the pop genre, songs such as "Gold" by Imagine Dragons convey deeper meanings, using gold as a symbol of personal worth, resilience, and the pursuit of happiness amid life's challenges. This duality—where gold represents both aspiration and critique—illustrates the complexity of contemporary culture's relationship with wealth.

The connection between gold and music is also evident in award ceremonies. The Grammy Awards, for instance, feature gold-plated trophies symbolizing artistic achievement, reinforcing gold's status as the pinnacle of success in the music industry. Winning a Grammy often elevates artists, lending them not just prestige but also commercial viability, demonstrating how gold functions as a tangible representation of accomplishment.

Gold's influence extends beyond music into broader entertainment spheres, including film and television. The Academy Awards, often referred to as the Oscars, present winners with gold statuettes, underscoring the connection between the film industry and the allure of gold. Movies often depict gold as a central theme, whether through narratives of treasure hunting, such as in "Indiana Jones," or as symbols of greed and corruption, as seen in "The Gold Rush" or "The Treasure of the Sierra Madre." These cinematic portrayals reflect societal fascinations and fears surrounding wealth, often highlighting the moral dilemmas associated with the pursuit of gold.

Moreover, gold has become a recurring motif in advertising and branding. Luxury brands frequently employ gold accents in their marketing strategies to evoke a sense of exclusivity and opulence. This is evident in campaigns for high-end products, jewelry, and even automobiles, where gold signifies not just quality, but also an aspirational lifestyle that many consumers desire.

In essence, gold's prevalence in music and entertainment underscores its multifaceted role in contemporary society. It serves as a potent symbol of aspiration, a marker of achievement, and a reflection of cultural values and critiques. The portrayal of gold—from the bling of hip-hop artists to the glittering awards of the entertainment industry—illustrates its enduring appeal and significance in shaping identity and narrative in modern culture. As society continues to evolve, so too will the meanings and representations of gold, ensuring its place as a timeless icon in the landscape of music and entertainment.

Gold in Sports: Trophies, Medals, and Glory

The symbolism of gold in sports transcends mere material value; it embodies the pinnacle of achievement, excellence, and victory. Historically, gold has been the ultimate prize in competitive sports, representing not just the highest honor but also the culmination of years of dedication, training, and sacrifice. This association can be traced back to ancient civilizations, where gold was used to craft trophies and awards, signifying triumph and success.

The Use of Gold Medals

One of the most recognized symbols of achievement in modern sports is the gold medal, awarded to first-place finishers in major competitions such as the Olympics. The tradition of awarding gold medals dates back to the 1900 Paris Olympics, where winners were honored with gold-plated medals. The significance of the gold medal is rooted in the historical context of the Olympic Games, which were originally held in ancient Greece to celebrate athletic prowess and honor the gods. The gold medal represents not only victory but also the athletes' hard work and commitment to their sport.

In addition to the Olympic Games, various international competitions, including the FIFA World Cup, the UEFA European Championship, and numerous world championships across different sports, feature gold medals as the highest accolade. Winning a gold medal often serves as a benchmark for athletes, solidifying their status in the annals of sporting history. The emotional weight carried by a gold medal transcends its physical composition, as it becomes a lifelong symbol of personal achievement and national pride.

Trophies: The Golden Icons of Sport

Beyond medals, gold is also prominently featured in the design of trophies awarded in various sports. Prestigious tournaments like the Wimbledon trophy in tennis, the Stanley Cup in hockey, and the FIFA World Cup trophy are crafted from gold or gold-plated materials, reinforcing the connection between gold and victory. These trophies serve as tangible reminders of an athlete's or team's success and are often displayed with pride, further enhancing their legacy.

The visual appeal of gold enhances the trophy's allure. The gleaming surface of a gold trophy not only signifies victory but also shines as a symbol of hard work and determination. For many athletes, hoisting a golden trophy above their heads is more than just a moment of celebration; it is a dream realized, often representing years of struggle and perseverance.

Cultural Significance and Legacy

The cultural significance of gold in sports extends beyond the individual athlete. Nations celebrate Olympic victories by honoring their gold medalists with parades, ceremonies, and national recognition, as these achievements foster a sense of community and national pride. The triumph of an athlete can inspire generations, while the stories behind their victories often become woven into the fabric of national identity.

Moreover, gold in sports can also reflect broader themes of social and economic status. Athletes who win gold medals often gain celebrity status, attracting sponsorships and endorsements, which further amplifies the connection between gold and success in the public eye. This dynamic emphasizes the dual role of gold in sports: as a representation of individual achievement and as a marker of societal recognition.

Conclusion
In conclusion, gold's role in sports as trophies, medals, and symbols of glory is profound. It encapsulates the essence of competition, victory, and human aspiration. The allure of gold inspires athletes to push their limits, striving for excellence while serving as a reminder of the enduring human spirit. As long as sports exist, the symbolism of gold will remain an integral part of the narrative surrounding achievement and glory, continuing to captivate and inspire both athletes and fans alike.

The Representation of Gold in Film and Media
Gold, often associated with wealth, power, and beauty, has played a significant role in film and media, serving not only as a plot device but also as a symbol of deeper societal themes. Its representation varies widely, reflecting cultural attitudes, historical contexts, and individual desires. This section explores how gold is portrayed in movies, television, and various media forms, highlighting its multifaceted significance.

Symbol of Wealth and Power
One of the most prominent representations of gold in film and media is as a symbol of wealth and power. Classic films such as Goldfinger (1964) from the James Bond franchise epitomize this association. The villain, Auric Goldfinger, embodies the extremes of greed and obsession with gold, showcasing how the lust for wealth can lead to moral corruption and criminality. The film's iconic imagery, including the luxurious gold-painted woman, reinforces the idea that gold represents not just material wealth but also status and dominance.

In contrast, the The Great Gatsby (2013), based on F. Scott Fitzgerald's novel, utilizes gold to highlight the excess and moral decay of the Jazz Age. The opulent parties filled with gold decor serve as a backdrop to the characters' pursuit of the elusive American Dream, emphasizing the superficiality that often accompanies wealth. Here, gold becomes a visual representation of the characters' aspirations and the ultimate emptiness of their pursuits.

The Allure of Gold and Adventure

Gold frequently serves as a catalyst for adventure and conflict in storytelling. Films like Indiana Jones and the Last Crusade (1989) and The Treasure of the Sierra Madre (1948) illustrate how the search for gold can drive individuals to extreme measures. Indiana Jones's quest for the Holy Grail, often depicted with gold elements, intertwines mythology and treasure hunting, suggesting that the pursuit of gold is not merely about riches but also about legacy, history, and identity.

Conversely, The Treasure of the Sierra Madre delves into the darker side of gold hunting. The film portrays how the quest for gold can lead to paranoia, betrayal, and moral decay among the characters. The phrase "We don't need no stinkin' badges!" has become emblematic of the greed and lawlessness that accompany the search for gold, illustrating how wealth can corrupt even the most noble intentions.

Cultural Symbolism and Mythology

Gold's representation extends beyond mere wealth to encompass cultural symbolism and mythology. In Lord of the Rings, the One Ring—crafted from gold—serves as a powerful metaphor for the corrupting influence of wealth and power. The ring's ability to seduce and corrupt reflects societal fears about the consequences of greed. This portrayal resonates with audiences, showcasing gold as a double-edged sword: it can grant power but also bring destruction.

Television shows, such as Breaking Bad, use gold as a symbol of transformation and ambition. The character Walter White's transition from a mild-mannered chemistry teacher to a drug lord is visually represented through gold items, reinforcing themes of ambition, moral ambiguity, and the desire for wealth.

Modern Media and Gold's Digital Representation

In contemporary media, gold continues to symbolize wealth, but it also intersects with themes of technology and digital culture. Video games, such as Minecraft and World of Warcraft, incorporate gold as a currency and status symbol, representing not just wealth but also the power to unlock new experiences and capabilities within the game. This digital representation mirrors societal trends where gold is not only a physical commodity but also a virtual one.

Conclusion

In conclusion, gold's portrayal in film and media is rich and varied, reflecting cultural values, societal aspirations, and individual desires. Whether as a symbol of wealth and power, an impetus for adventure, or a representation of deeper moral dilemmas, gold captivates audiences and serves as a timeless motif that continues to resonate across genres and formats. As both a physical and symbolic element, gold remains a powerful narrative device that shapes our understanding of wealth, ambition, and the human experience.

The Psychological Appeal of Gold Today

Gold has been a coveted metal for millennia, with its allure transcending cultures, epochs, and economic systems. In the modern world, gold continues to captivate our collective imagination, serving not only as a tangible asset but also as a powerful symbol laden with psychological significance. This enduring appeal can be attributed to several factors, including its historical context, cultural symbolism, inherent properties, and its role in contemporary society.

Historical Context and Cultural Significance

Gold's allure is deeply rooted in its history. From ancient civilizations that revered it as a divine substance to its use in currency and trade, gold has consistently symbolized wealth, power, and status. Historical narratives surrounding gold—from the myths of El Dorado to the opulence of royal treasuries—have ingrained it in our collective psyche as a representation of human aspiration and achievement. This historical significance continues to inform how modern society perceives gold; it is not merely a commodity but a vessel of stories and human endeavor.

Symbol of Wealth and Success

In contemporary culture, gold is often associated with affluence and success. The phrase "the golden touch" evokes the idea of effortless wealth creation, while gold jewelry remains a quintessential symbol of status and prestige. The use of gold in awards—such as Olympic medals—further reinforces its association with triumph and excellence. This connection prompts individuals to aspire to acquire gold, not just for its monetary value but for the social validation it provides. As people navigate a complex world characterized by fluctuating economic conditions, gold stands as a reassuring symbol of stability and permanence.

Inherent Properties and Aesthetic Appeal

Gold possesses unique physical and chemical properties that contribute to its desirability. It is durable, malleable, and resistant to tarnish, which makes it ideal for crafting jewelry and artifacts that can withstand the test of time. Its brilliant luster and warm color evoke feelings of beauty and luxury. In a world increasingly driven by digital transactions and ephemeral experiences, the tangible nature of gold offers a sense of physical security. Holding a gold coin or wearing gold jewelry can elicit a visceral connection to wealth that is both satisfying and affirming.

Investment and Economic Security

In modern finance, gold is often viewed as a "safe haven" asset, a refuge in times of economic uncertainty. When markets are volatile, investors frequently turn to gold, believing it will retain its value better than currencies or stocks. This perception is not unfounded; gold has historically held its value over long periods, often appreciating when other investments falter. The psychological comfort derived from owning gold as part of a diversified portfolio reinforces its status as a reliable asset, further enhancing its appeal.

Cultural Representations and Media Influence

The portrayal of gold in media—films, music, and literature—continues to shape public perception. Gold is often depicted as a symbol of allure and danger, intertwined with themes of greed and ambition. Such representations tap into the duality of gold: it is both a coveted treasure and a potential source of conflict. This complex narrative adds layers to its psychological appeal, making gold a multifaceted symbol in the modern imagination.

Conclusion

The psychological appeal of gold today is a confluence of its historical significance, cultural symbolism, aesthetic properties, economic role, and media portrayals. As society evolves, so too does the narrative surrounding gold. It remains a timeless object of desire, rooted in our collective consciousness, representing not only wealth and power but also the aspirations, fears, and dreams of humanity. This enduring fascination is likely to persist, as gold continues to inspire and captivate the modern imagination, embodying both our past and our future.

Chapter 14

Gold and Technology

Gold in Ancient Technology

Gold, revered for its beauty, malleability, and resistance to tarnish, has been associated with wealth and power since ancient times. However, its significance extends far beyond mere ornamentation and currency; it played a crucial role in early technological innovations across various cultures. This section explores how ancient civilizations harnessed gold's unique properties to advance technology, improve everyday life, and influence societal structures.

The Unique Properties of Gold

Gold is one of the least reactive chemical elements, which means it does not corrode or tarnish, making it an ideal material for long-lasting artifacts. Its malleability allows it to be easily shaped and worked into intricate designs, while its excellent conductivity makes it useful in early electrical experiments and applications. These properties set gold apart from other metals and made it a preferred choice for various technological applications in ancient societies.

Jewelry and Decorative Arts

One of the earliest applications of gold was in the creation of jewelry and decorative items. The craftsmanship of ancient goldsmiths, particularly in cultures such as those in Egypt, Mesopotamia, and the Indus Valley, showcased intricate techniques such as granulation, filigree, and inlay. This artistry not only served aesthetic purposes but also advanced techniques in metallurgy and metalworking. The skills developed in these early practices laid the groundwork for more complex technological advancements in later periods.

Gold in Medicine

In addition to decorative uses, gold was employed in early medicine. Ancient Egyptians, for example, utilized gold in various medicinal applications, believing it possessed healing properties. Gold foils were used in plasters and poultices, while some texts suggest that gold was even ingested in powdered form to treat ailments. The use of gold in medical practices reflects an early understanding of the metal's biocompatibility and non-reactive nature, paving the way for its later applications in modern medicine.

Electrical Conductivity and Early Experiments
Gold's excellent conductivity was recognized even in ancient times, albeit in a rudimentary form. The ancient Greeks, particularly philosophers like Thales of Miletus, experimented with static electricity and magnetism. Although they did not have the technology to fully exploit these properties, the foundational ideas about electrical phenomena were emerging. Gold's role in these early experiments hinted at its future applications in electronics and technology.

Religious and Cultural Significance
In many ancient cultures, gold held a sacred status, often associated with the divine. This reverence led to technological advancements in religious artifacts, such as the creation of elaborate altars, statues, and ceremonial objects. The Egyptians, for example, used gold extensively in burial practices, believing it would accompany the deceased into the afterlife. This not only showcased their advanced metalworking skills but also reflected a societal structure that prioritized religious and cultural expressions through technology.

Early Coinage and Trade
Gold's introduction as a medium for coinage marked a significant technological and economic advancement. The Lydians are credited with minting the first gold coins around 600 BCE, which standardized trade and facilitated commerce. This innovation transformed economic systems and prompted the development of banking and financial institutions, showcasing how gold's properties were leveraged to create a reliable and trusted medium of exchange.

Conclusion
Gold's early applications in technology were diverse and impactful, influencing various aspects of ancient life and culture. From exquisite jewelry to medicinal uses, and from religious artifacts to the birth of coinage, gold's unique properties catalyzed significant advancements in technology. These foundational innovations not only shaped ancient societies but also laid the groundwork for future developments in metallurgy, medicine, and economics, illustrating the enduring legacy of gold in human history.

Gold in Modern Electronics: Essential and Irreplaceable
Gold is often celebrated for its beauty and historical significance as a symbol of wealth, but in the realm of modern electronics, its unique properties make it an essential component of contemporary technological devices. This precious metal plays a crucial role in various electronic applications due to its exceptional conductivity, resistance to corrosion, and malleability.

Electrical Conductivity

One of the primary reasons for gold's prevalence in electronic devices is its unparalleled electrical conductivity. Gold is one of the best conductors of electricity, surpassed only by copper and silver, but it offers substantial advantages in specific applications. For instance, gold's resistance to tarnishing and corrosion ensures that electrical connections remain reliable over time, even in harsh environments. This is particularly important in high-precision devices such as smartphones, computers, and medical equipment, where even a slight degradation in performance can lead to significant operational failures.

Connectors and Contacts

Gold is widely used for connectors, switches, and other components that require a reliable and durable electrical connection. In many devices, gold plating is applied to connectors and contact points to enhance conductivity and prevent oxidation. This gold plating is often found in the connectors of audio equipment, high-definition video interfaces, and various computing components. The use of gold in these applications not only improves performance but also extends the lifespan of devices, contributing to sustainability by reducing the need for frequent replacements.

Circuit Boards

In circuit boards, gold is utilized in several forms, including gold-plated pads and traces. These components are critical for ensuring efficient signal transmission and minimizing electrical resistance. The integration of gold in circuit boards can be particularly advantageous in high-frequency applications, such as telecommunications and data transmission, where signal integrity is paramount. Moreover, the durability of gold helps safeguard the circuit boards against environmental factors, ensuring long-term reliability.

Semiconductor Applications

Gold's role extends into the realm of semiconductors, where it is employed in wire bonding and interconnection processes. In semiconductor manufacturing, tiny gold wires are used to connect integrated circuits to their packages, facilitating the flow of electrical signals. This is especially vital in advanced technologies like microprocessors and memory chips, which form the backbone of modern computing and data storage solutions. The ability of gold to bond effectively with silicon and other materials further enhances its utility in this field.

Emerging Technologies

As technology evolves, the demand for gold in electronics is expected to grow. The rise of devices such as wearables, IoT (Internet of Things) devices, and electric vehicles presents new opportunities for gold utilization. For instance, the miniaturization of components in wearable technology often requires materials that maintain high performance in limited spaces—properties that gold readily provides. Additionally, the automotive industry is increasingly integrating electronic systems that benefit from gold's conductive properties, particularly in electric vehicles and advanced driver-assistance systems (ADAS).

Sustainability and Recycling
The electronic industry is also recognizing the importance of sustainability. Gold is recyclable, making it a valuable material in efforts to reduce electronic waste. Recycling gold from old devices not only conserves natural resources but also minimizes the environmental impact associated with gold mining. As the industry shifts toward more sustainable practices, the role of recycled gold in electronics is likely to become more significant.

Conclusion
In conclusion, gold's essential role in modern electronics stems from its unique properties that enhance the performance, reliability, and longevity of electronic devices. As technology continues to advance, gold will remain irreplaceable, ensuring that our devices operate efficiently while also contributing to sustainability through recycling initiatives. The integration of gold in contemporary electronics not only underscores its versatility but also highlights its ongoing importance in shaping the future of technology.

The Future of Gold in Nanotechnology
As we navigate the complexities of the 21st century, gold continues to hold a pivotal role, not just as a symbol of wealth and status, but also as a critical material in the rapidly evolving field of nanotechnology. This intersection of gold and nanotechnology is opening new frontiers in various sectors, including medicine, electronics, and environmental science. The unique properties of gold at the nanoscale make it an invaluable asset for innovative applications that promise to revolutionize how we approach some of the most pressing challenges of our time.

Unique Properties of Gold Nanoparticles
Gold nanoparticles (AuNPs) exhibit distinctive characteristics that differ from their bulk counterparts, primarily due to the high surface area-to-volume ratio and quantum effects. At the nanoscale, gold can exhibit varying colors and enhanced reactivity, which can be finely tuned by altering particle size, shape, and surface chemistry. These properties make gold nanoparticles highly versatile and suitable for a diverse array of applications.

Applications in Medicine
One of the most promising applications of gold in nanotechnology is in the field of medicine, particularly in drug delivery and diagnostics. Gold nanoparticles can be engineered to carry

therapeutic agents directly to target cells, reducing side effects and improving treatment efficacy. For instance, their ability to absorb light allows for photothermal therapy, in which nanoparticles are localized to cancer cells and heated to destroy them without harming surrounding tissues.

Moreover, gold nanoparticles are increasingly being used in biosensors for early disease detection. Their surface can be functionalized with biomolecules that specifically bind to diseases, allowing for highly sensitive detection of pathogens or cancer biomarkers. This capability not only enhances diagnostic accuracy but also facilitates rapid testing, which is crucial in managing public health crises.

Advancements in Electronics

In the realm of electronics, gold's excellent conductivity and resistance to oxidation make it an ideal candidate for the development of next-generation devices. Gold nanoparticles are being integrated into flexible electronic devices, enhancing performance while maintaining lightweight and compact designs. This application is particularly relevant for wearable technology, where the demand for both functionality and comfort is paramount.

Additionally, gold is being explored for use in quantum computing, where its properties could aid in the development of qubits, the fundamental units of quantum information. The potential for gold to improve the efficiency of quantum systems could have significant implications for computing power and data processing.

Environmental Applications

Sustainability is another critical area where gold nanoparticles are making an impact. Their unique catalytic properties are being harnessed in environmental remediation efforts, such as the breakdown of pollutants in water. Gold nanoparticles can be utilized to catalyze reactions that convert harmful substances into less toxic forms, thereby contributing to cleaner water sources.

Furthermore, researchers are investigating gold's role in solar energy applications. Gold nanoparticles can enhance the efficiency of solar cells by improving light absorption and conversion, thus supporting the transition to renewable energy sources.

Challenges and Future Directions

Despite the promising applications of gold in nanotechnology, several challenges remain. The cost of gold, while historically stable, poses a barrier to widespread adoption, particularly in low-cost applications. Additionally, concerns regarding the environmental impact of gold mining and the long-term effects of introducing nanoparticles into ecosystems necessitate further research and sustainable practices.

As the field of nanotechnology continues to mature, collaboration between scientists, engineers, and industry leaders will be essential in overcoming these obstacles. The future of gold in nanotechnology is bright, with the potential to drive innovations that not only enhance human health and technological capabilities but also contribute to a more sustainable future. The ongoing research and development in this area will undoubtedly expand our understanding of gold's unique properties and unlock new opportunities for its application across various sectors.

Innovations in Gold Recycling: A Sustainable Future

As global awareness of environmental issues intensifies, the gold industry is increasingly focusing on sustainability, particularly through the advancement of recycling methods. Gold recycling not only conserves natural resources but also significantly reduces the ecological footprint associated with traditional gold mining. Innovations in technology have played a pivotal role in enhancing the efficiency and effectiveness of gold recycling processes, paving the way for a more sustainable future.

The Importance of Gold Recycling

Gold recycling is crucial for several reasons. First and foremost, gold is a finite resource, and traditional mining can lead to significant environmental degradation, including deforestation, soil erosion, and water pollution. Recycling helps mitigate these impacts by extending the lifecycle of existing gold, reducing the demand for newly mined gold. Moreover, as the value of gold continues to rise, recycling becomes an economically attractive option, enabling industries to reclaim precious metals from obsolete products.

Technological Innovations in Gold Recycling

Recent technological advancements have revolutionized the gold recycling process in various ways:

1. Hydrometallurgical Methods: One of the most significant innovations is the development of hydrometallurgical techniques, which utilize aqueous solutions to dissolve and recover gold from electronic waste (e-waste) and other scrap materials. This method is less harmful to the environment compared to traditional pyrometallurgical techniques that involve high-temperature smelting. Hydrometallurgical processes are particularly effective in extracting gold from complex matrices, such as circuit boards, through selective leaching agents that target gold without damaging other valuable materials.

2. Biotechnology: The integration of biotechnology into gold recycling offers a promising avenue for sustainable practices. Researchers are exploring the use of bioleaching, which employs microorganisms to extract metals from ores or waste products. Certain bacteria can metabolize and solubilize gold, making it feasible to recover it from electronic waste or tailings. This approach not only minimizes environmental harm but also reduces the energy consumption typically associated with traditional extraction methods.

3. Advanced Sorting Technologies: Innovations in sorting technologies, such as X-ray fluorescence (XRF) and laser-induced breakdown spectroscopy (LIBS), have improved the efficiency of gold recovery from scrap materials. These techniques allow for rapid, non-destructive analysis of materials, enabling recyclers to identify and separate gold-containing components from other materials with great precision. This technological leap reduces processing time and enhances the purity of the recovered gold.

4. Closed-Loop Recycling: The concept of closed-loop recycling, where materials are continuously recycled back into the production cycle, is gaining traction in the gold industry. By implementing systems that recapture and reuse gold within manufacturing processes, companies can minimize waste and decrease their reliance on newly mined gold. Innovations in design for recycling (DfR) are also crucial, as they help manufacturers create products that are easier to disassemble and recycle at the end of their life cycle.

5. Blockchain Technology: Transparency and traceability in the recycling process are essential to ensure the ethical sourcing of recycled gold. Blockchain technology is emerging as a solution to track the journey of gold from recycling facilities to end-users. By providing an immutable record of transactions, blockchain can help assure consumers that the gold they purchase is sourced responsibly and sustainably, further incentivizing recycling practices.

Conclusion

The innovations in gold recycling represent a significant shift towards sustainable practices in the gold industry. As technologies continue to evolve, the efficiency and effectiveness of recycling processes will only improve, contributing to resource conservation and environmental protection. By embracing these advancements, the industry can reduce its ecological footprint while meeting the ever-growing demand for gold in a responsible manner. Ultimately, innovations in gold recycling not only support sustainability but also foster a circular economy, where gold remains a valued resource for generations to come.

The Potential for Gold in Renewable Energy

As the world grapples with the pressing need for sustainable energy solutions, the role of materials in facilitating the transition to renewable energy sources has gained significant importance. Among these materials, gold stands out for its unique properties and potential applications in various aspects of energy generation, storage, and efficiency.

Gold's Unique Properties

Gold is renowned for its exceptional conductivity, resistance to corrosion, and malleability, making it an invaluable resource in the realm of electronics and energy technologies. These properties not only enhance the performance of devices but also contribute to the longevity and reliability of renewable energy systems.

For instance, gold's conductivity plays a crucial role in solar energy technologies. In photovoltaic cells, which convert sunlight into electricity, gold can be used in the form of thin films or nanoparticles to improve light absorption and enhance the efficiency of the cells. Research has shown that incorporating gold nanoparticles into solar cell designs can significantly increase their power conversion efficiency. This enhancement is particularly beneficial in the quest for more efficient solar panels that meet global energy demands.

Applications in Energy Storage

Gold also holds promise in the field of energy storage, particularly in lithium-ion batteries, which are widely used in electric vehicles and renewable energy systems. The integration of gold into battery technology can improve the performance of these batteries by enhancing their charge-discharge rates and overall lifespan. Researchers have explored the use of gold as a catalyst in battery reactions, which can lead to faster charging times and higher energy densities.

Furthermore, gold's stability in diverse environments makes it an excellent candidate for developing new battery chemistries. As the demand for more efficient and durable energy storage solutions grows, gold's role in advancing battery technology could prove pivotal in supporting the widespread adoption of renewable energy sources.

Gold in Fuel Cells

Fuel cells are another area where gold can make a significant impact. These devices convert chemical energy directly into electricity through electrochemical reactions, and they are increasingly seen as a clean alternative to traditional combustion engines. Gold can be used as a catalyst in fuel cell reactions, specifically in proton exchange membrane fuel cells (PEMFCs), which are known for their efficiency and low environmental impact.

The use of gold catalysts can enhance the performance of PEMFCs by reducing the amount of precious metals required, thus lowering production costs while maintaining high efficiency. As countries strive to reduce their carbon footprints, the adoption of fuel cells powered by renewable hydrogen becomes more feasible with advancements in gold-based catalysts.

The Future of Gold in Renewable Energy

While the potential for gold in renewable energy systems is promising, the industry must also consider the environmental implications of gold mining and production. Sustainable mining practices, recycling, and the development of eco-friendly extraction technologies are essential to ensure that the use of gold in renewable energy does not exacerbate environmental degradation. The push for ethically sourced gold, including efforts to recycle gold from electronic waste, can contribute to a circular economy where the benefits of gold are realized without compromising ecological integrity.

Additionally, as the renewable energy landscape continues to evolve, ongoing research and innovation will be critical in unlocking the full potential of gold within this sector. Collaborations between scientists, engineers, and industry stakeholders can drive the development of new technologies that leverage gold's unique properties for sustainable energy solutions.

Conclusion

In summary, gold possesses remarkable qualities that position it as a key material in advancing renewable energy technologies. From enhancing the efficiency of solar panels to improving battery storage and fuel cell performance, gold's potential contributions to sustainable energy solutions are vast. However, the industry must navigate the challenges associated with gold extraction and usage responsibly to ensure that its role in the renewable energy sector is both beneficial and sustainable. As the world shifts towards greener energy solutions, gold may well play a crucial part in shaping a more sustainable future.

Chapter 15

Gold and the Future of Money

The Debate Over Returning to the Gold Standard

The gold standard, a monetary system in which a country's currency or paper money has a value directly linked to gold, was once the foundation of international finance. Its historical significance and the debate surrounding its potential return are both complex and multifaceted, reflecting differing economic ideologies and values.

Historical Context

The gold standard was widely adopted in the 19th and early 20th centuries, providing a stable monetary framework that facilitated global trade and investment. However, the economic upheaval of the Great Depression and the subsequent abandonment of the gold standard during the 1930s led to its gradual decline. By the early 1970s, the United States officially left the gold standard, moving towards fiat currency systems, where the value of money is not backed by physical commodities but rather by government decree.

Pros of Returning to the Gold Standard

1. Stability and Predictability: Proponents argue that a return to the gold standard would provide greater stability for economies. By limiting the amount of money that can be printed to the amount of gold held, it could help prevent inflation, which erodes purchasing power and savings. A gold-backed currency can instill confidence among investors and consumers, as the intrinsic value of gold acts as a safeguard against reckless monetary policy.

2. Discipline in Monetary Policy: Adopting the gold standard could impose strict limits on government spending and borrowing. This fiscal discipline might mitigate excessive national debt and promote balanced budgets, as governments would need to maintain sufficient gold reserves to support their currency.

3. Long-term Value: Gold has historically maintained its value over time, making it an attractive store of wealth. Advocates posit that a gold standard could help stabilize currencies in the face of economic shocks, creating a more resilient financial system.

Cons of Returning to the Gold Standard

1. Limited Monetary Flexibility: Critics argue that a gold standard restricts a government's ability to respond to economic crises. In times of recession or financial instability, the ability to implement monetary stimulus—such as adjusting interest rates or increasing the money supply—becomes constrained. This limitation could exacerbate economic downturns, leading to prolonged periods of recession.

2. Gold Supply Issues: The amount of gold available is finite and can be subject to significant fluctuations due to mining yields and geopolitical factors. A currency system reliant on gold may face challenges in responding to economic growth or contraction, as the gold supply may not align with the needs of a dynamically changing economy.

3. Transition Costs and Risks: Returning to a gold standard would involve substantial transition costs, including the potential for significant disruptions in current financial systems. The complexities of establishing a new monetary framework, along with the risk of speculative attacks on currencies tied to gold, could lead to economic instability during the transition.

Conclusion
The debate over returning to the gold standard reflects broader discussions about the nature of money, the role of government in the economy, and the balance between stability and flexibility in monetary policy. While a gold-backed currency system may offer benefits in terms of stability and discipline, the potential drawbacks—particularly regarding economic flexibility and the practicality of implementation—pose significant challenges. As economies continue to evolve and face new financial realities, the discussion surrounding the gold standard remains a compelling topic for economists, policymakers, and the public alike.

Cryptocurrency vs. Gold: The New Digital Gold Rush?

The emergence of cryptocurrencies, particularly Bitcoin, has ignited a fervent debate regarding the future of money and the role of traditional assets like gold. Both gold and cryptocurrencies serve as stores of value, yet they embody fundamentally different characteristics, usage scenarios, and underlying philosophies. This section explores the comparison between gold and cryptocurrencies, the implications of this "digital gold rush," and the potential for both assets in the evolving financial landscape.

Historical Context and Value Proposition
Gold has been revered for thousands of years as a symbol of wealth and stability. Its intrinsic properties—scarcity, durability, and divisibility—have made it a reliable store of value. Gold's

historical role as a currency and its backing of various monetary systems further solidify its status in the financial world. In contrast, Bitcoin, launched in 2009, was created as a decentralized digital currency that operates on blockchain technology. It was designed to be a digital alternative to fiat currencies and has gained traction as a speculative asset.

Scarcity and Supply Dynamics
Gold is a finite resource, with annual production varying but typically around 3,000 metric tons. New gold mining ventures can take years to develop, creating a relatively stable supply. Conversely, Bitcoin has a capped supply of 21 million coins, which creates a scarcity that is mathematically enforced through its coded protocol. New Bitcoins are mined at a decreasing rate through a process called halving, which occurs approximately every four years, mimicking gold's scarcity, but with a predetermined and transparent issuance schedule.

Volatility and Investment Behavior
The price of gold tends to be less volatile than that of cryptocurrencies. Gold's value fluctuates based on global economic conditions, inflation rates, and geopolitical stability. In contrast, Bitcoin and other cryptocurrencies exhibit extreme price volatility, often experiencing substantial short-term swings. This volatility attracts speculative investors looking for high returns, but it also raises concerns about the reliability of cryptocurrencies as a stable store of value.

Regulatory Landscape and Acceptance
Gold enjoys a long-standing acceptance in global markets, recognized as a safe-haven asset during times of economic uncertainty. Its regulatory framework is well-established, providing some assurance to investors. Cryptocurrencies, on the other hand, face a shifting regulatory environment that varies significantly across countries. This uncertainty can lead to concerns about the future viability of digital currencies and their potential for mainstream adoption.

Technological Factors and Accessibility
The digital nature of cryptocurrencies allows for instantaneous transactions, lower transfer costs, and greater accessibility to global markets. Individuals can buy, sell, and trade cryptocurrencies easily through various platforms, making them appealing to a tech-savvy population. However, this also creates vulnerabilities, such as cyberattacks and loss of access to digital wallets. Gold, while less convenient for daily transactions, remains a tangible asset that can be physically held, which appeals to traditional investors seeking security.

Cultural Perceptions and Psychological Factors
Gold carries deep cultural significance, often associated with wealth, beauty, and tradition. Its allure is ingrained in human history, symbolizing prosperity and power. Conversely, cryptocurrencies are often viewed with skepticism by the mainstream, seen as speculative or even risky investments. However, as younger generations become more comfortable with digital assets, the perception of cryptocurrencies is gradually shifting, fostering a new cultural landscape where digital assets could coexist with traditional assets like gold.

Conclusion: The Future of Value
As the world increasingly embraces digital innovation, the relationship between gold and cryptocurrencies continues to evolve. While gold remains a time-honored asset with a proven track record, the rise of cryptocurrencies presents a compelling narrative of financial evolution. Investors may increasingly view Bitcoin and other cryptocurrencies as a new form of "digital gold," particularly as a hedge against inflation and currency devaluation. Ultimately, the future of both assets will likely be shaped by ongoing technological advancements, regulatory developments, and shifts in investor sentiment, creating a complex interplay between ancient and modern forms of value.

The Role of Gold in a Cashless Society
As societies globally transition towards cashless economies, driven by advancements in technology and changing consumer behaviors, the role of traditional currencies is being fundamentally redefined. In this evolving landscape, gold—an ancient symbol of wealth and value—may still find relevance, even as digital transactions become the norm. Understanding how gold could function in a cashless society requires an exploration of its historical significance, intrinsic properties, and potential modern applications.

The Historical Context of Gold
Gold has been revered for millennia as a reliable store of value, a medium of exchange, and a symbol of wealth. Its scarcity, durability, divisibility, and fungibility make it a desirable asset across cultures and epochs. While fiat currencies have emerged as the primary means of transaction, gold has retained its status as a hedge against inflation and economic instability. In times of financial crisis, gold often acts as a safe haven, prompting investors to flock to its perceived stability. This historical context suggests that even in a cashless society, gold's intrinsic value may continue to offer a counterbalance to the volatility of digital currencies.

Gold as a Digital Asset
In a cashless society, the digitization of gold could facilitate its integration into modern financial systems. Digital gold, represented as a cryptocurrency or a blockchain-based asset, would allow

individuals to buy, sell, and trade gold efficiently without the need for physical transfer. This digital representation could ensure that ownership is easily verifiable, secure, and accessible, mirroring the principles that underpin cryptocurrencies like Bitcoin. By digitizing gold, it can be seamlessly incorporated into digital wallets, enabling users to transact in gold alongside traditional currencies or cryptocurrencies.

Gold-Backed Digital Currencies

Another potential role for gold in a cashless society is through the establishment of gold-backed digital currencies. Central banks and financial institutions could issue currencies that are partially or fully backed by gold reserves. This would provide a tangible asset to bolster confidence in digital currency systems, combining the advantages of modern payment methods with the stability of gold. Such currencies could serve as a bridge between traditional monetary systems and the rapidly evolving landscape of digital finance, providing reassurance to users that their digital assets have inherent value.

The Psychological Appeal of Gold

Gold's enduring allure lies not just in its physical properties but also in its psychological significance. In a world increasingly dominated by abstract digital transactions, the tactile and historical weight of gold may provide a sense of security and permanence. As individuals navigate the complexities of a cashless society, the emotional connection to gold could drive demand for its inclusion in financial portfolios and as a form of wealth preservation. This psychological factor might encourage individuals to seek gold not only as an investment but also as a safeguard against the unpredictability of digital currencies.

Challenges and Considerations

While gold's integration into a cashless society presents opportunities, several challenges must be addressed. The logistics of securely storing and transporting gold, regulatory frameworks governing digital assets, and potential market volatility are just a few of the issues that need careful consideration. Additionally, public awareness and understanding of digital gold and gold-backed currencies will be crucial in fostering acceptance and trust among consumers.

Conclusion

As we move towards an increasingly cashless society, gold may play a multifaceted role that transcends its traditional applications. By leveraging modern technology to digitize gold and create gold-backed digital currencies, we can bridge the gap between historical value and contemporary financial systems. Gold's unique properties and psychological significance may ensure its relevance in a future dominated by digital transactions, serving as a timeless asset that continues to captivate and provide stability in the evolving economic landscape.

The Global Shift Toward Digital Gold

In recent years, a significant transformation has emerged in the way gold is perceived, owned, and traded, largely driven by advancements in digital technologies. The concept of "digital gold" encapsulates this shift, where traditional physical gold is increasingly being represented and traded in digital formats. This evolution presents a myriad of implications for investors, traders, and the broader financial ecosystem.

The Emergence of Digital Gold

Digital gold refers to a method of investing in gold without the necessity of physical possession. This can take several forms, including gold-backed cryptocurrencies, digital gold accounts, and tokenized gold assets. Platforms such as VaultChain and Tether Gold allow users to buy and trade gold that is securely stored in vaults, with ownership represented through digital tokens. This development not only streamlines the trading process but also lowers the barriers to entry for individual investors. With the click of a button, users can trade gold as easily as they would cryptocurrencies or stocks.

Advantages of Digital Gold

One of the most significant advantages of digital gold is its liquidity. Traditional gold trading can involve cumbersome processes, including shipping and storage, which can deter potential investors. Digital gold eliminates these logistical challenges, allowing for instant transactions. This increased liquidity makes it easier for investors to buy and sell gold rapidly, responding to market fluctuations in real-time.

Moreover, digital gold can often be traded 24/7 on various platforms, unlike traditional commodity exchanges that operate on set hours. This around-the-clock availability aligns with the global nature of finance today, where investors across different time zones can engage with the gold market at their convenience.

Transparency and Security

Blockchain technology has further enhanced the credibility of digital gold. The transparency and immutability of blockchain allow for secure ownership records, minimizing the risks associated with fraud or misrepresentation that can occur in the physical gold market. Each transaction is recorded on a public ledger, which ensures that all holders of digital gold can verify their ownership and the authenticity of the asset. This transparency is particularly appealing to younger, tech-savvy investors who prioritize trust and security in their financial dealings.

Investment Diversification and Accessibility

Digital gold also democratizes access to gold as an investment. Traditional gold ownership often requires significant capital, with costs including not only the price of the gold itself but also storage fees and insurance. Digital platforms can offer fractional ownership, allowing investors to purchase smaller amounts of gold, thus making it more accessible. This fractionalization enables a wider audience to diversify their portfolios with gold, a historical safe-haven asset, without needing substantial upfront investment.

The Rise of Gold-Backed Cryptocurrencies

The intersection of gold and blockchain has led to the rise of gold-backed cryptocurrencies, which are designed to combine the stability of gold with the flexibility of digital currencies. These tokens are typically pegged to physical gold reserves, offering a transparent and liquid means of owning gold. This innovation has attracted both cryptocurrency enthusiasts and traditional investors seeking a hedge against economic instability, inflation, or currency devaluation.

Challenges and Future Outlook

Despite the advantages, the shift toward digital gold also comes with challenges. Concerns regarding regulatory oversight, market volatility, and the technological infrastructure necessary for widespread adoption must be addressed. Regulatory bodies are still figuring out how to best manage digital assets, which could impact the future growth of digital gold markets.

In conclusion, the global shift toward digital gold reflects the ongoing integration of technology within financial systems. As digital platforms evolve and gain acceptance, they promise to reshape the landscape of gold ownership and trading, making it more accessible, efficient, and secure than ever before. This transformation underscores a broader trend where traditional assets are increasingly being digitized, paving the way for a new era in investment and commerce. As technology continues to advance, the future of gold—both physical and digital—seems poised for significant change, blending the allure of this ancient precious metal with the innovations of the digital age.

Gold as a Universal Currency: A Timeless Standard?

Throughout history, gold has been revered not only as a precious metal but also as a universal currency and a store of value. Its unique properties—scarcity, divisibility, durability, and intrinsic beauty—have established it as a reliable medium of exchange and a symbol of wealth. In an era increasingly dominated by digital currencies and fiat money, the question arises: will gold retain its status as a universal store of value?

Historical Context

Gold's role as a currency dates back thousands of years. Ancient civilizations, including the Egyptians, Greeks, and Romans, used gold coins as a standard means of trade. The metal's intrinsic value and acceptance across various cultures facilitated international trade and economic stability. Even during periods of economic turmoil, gold has acted as a safe haven, maintaining its worth when fiat currencies falter.

The establishment of the gold standard in the 19th century further solidified gold's status as a universal currency. Under this system, currencies were directly linked to gold, ensuring that governments could exchange paper money for a specific amount of gold. This linkage provided a level of trust and stability in monetary systems globally.

Contemporary Relevance

In today's economy, the dynamics have changed significantly with the rise of fiat currencies and digital payment systems. Central banks no longer strictly adhere to the gold standard, allowing for greater flexibility in monetary policy. However, the intrinsic qualities of gold as a hedge against inflation and currency devaluation continue to resonate with investors and governments alike.

Gold's historical performance as a store of value is particularly relevant during economic downturns. For instance, during the 2008 financial crisis, many investors flocked to gold, driving up its price as a safe haven asset. This behavior suggests that even in a digital age, gold retains its allure as a protective asset against economic instability.

The Role of Digital Currencies

The emergence of cryptocurrencies, such as Bitcoin, has sparked a debate about the future of gold as a store of value. Proponents of cryptocurrencies argue that they offer a decentralized alternative to traditional forms of currency, potentially displacing gold's long-held supremacy. However, while cryptocurrencies share some characteristics with gold—such as scarcity and the ability to facilitate trade—they lack the historical track record and tangible nature that gold possesses.

Unlike digital currencies, gold is a physical asset that has been cherished across cultures for millennia. Its appeal is deeply rooted in human psychology, as evidenced by its depiction in art, religion, and culture. Furthermore, gold's physicality provides a level of security that digital currencies cannot guarantee, making it a more reliable store of value for many.

The Future of Gold
Looking ahead, several factors will influence gold's position as a universal currency. Economic uncertainties, geopolitical tensions, and shifts in monetary policy will likely reinforce gold's role as a safe haven. Additionally, the growing awareness of the environmental and ethical implications of mining may lead to increased focus on sustainable gold practices, further enhancing its desirability.

Moreover, the concept of "digital gold" has emerged, wherein gold is tokenized and traded on blockchain platforms. This innovation merges the stability of gold with the efficiency of digital transactions, potentially revitalizing gold's relevance in modern finance.

In conclusion, while the rise of digital currencies presents new challenges, gold is poised to maintain its status as a universal store of value. Its historical significance, intrinsic qualities, and enduring appeal ensure that it will continue to be a cornerstone of economic stability and a symbol of wealth in the 21st century. The timeless allure of gold, rooted in its unique properties and cultural significance, suggests that it will retain its status as a universal currency for generations to come.

Chapter 16

The Myths and Legends of Gold

The Myth of El Dorado: The City of Gold

The legend of El Dorado, often referred to as the "City of Gold," has captivated the imaginations of explorers, adventurers, and historians for centuries. The myth is rooted in the early European encounters with South America during the Age of Exploration, particularly focusing on the indigenous cultures of the region. Initially, El Dorado referred not to a specific city but to a king or a chief who was said to cover himself in gold dust and then plunge into Lake Guatavita as part of an elaborate ritual. This king, known as "El Dorado," became the focal point of myths that would evolve over time into the idea of an entire city made of gold.

The story of El Dorado emerged in the early 16th century against a backdrop of European expansion and conquest in the Americas. Following the Spanish conquest of the Aztec Empire, tales began to circulate about the wealth of South American civilizations. The Spanish conquistadors, driven by a relentless pursuit of gold, were eager to capitalize on these stories. The indigenous peoples, including the Muisca of present-day Colombia, spoke of a king who would adorn himself in gold and offer treasures to the gods, fueling the imaginations of the conquistadors.

The journey to find El Dorado became a quest that lured many explorers into the treacherous jungles and mountains of South America. Notable figures such as Gonzalo Pizarro and Francisco de Orellana embarked on expeditions that took them deep into the Amazon rainforest. These expeditions were often marked by hardship, internal conflict, and tragedy, yet they underscored the lengths to which people would go in the name of gold. Pizarro's expedition in the 1540s, for example, led to the brutal exploitation of indigenous peoples and the devastation of their cultures, driven by the insatiable European demand for gold.

Despite numerous expeditions, El Dorado remained elusive. As explorers returned empty-handed, the myth itself transformed. No longer just a king, El Dorado morphed into a city filled with unimaginable wealth, inspiring countless others to seek their fortune in the uncharted territories of the New World. The legend took on a life of its own, reflecting the hopes and dreams of those who sought to find not just material wealth but also a sense of adventure and discovery.

By the late 17th century, the myth had reached a point where the idea of El Dorado was synonymous with the broader concept of a "land of riches." It became a metaphor for unattainable wealth, embodying the notion of a dream that could lead to ruin. Many expeditions were launched under the banner of finding El Dorado, leading to further exploration of the Amazon basin and other regions, but most ended in failure or disaster. The obsession with the myth contributed to the tragic decline of numerous indigenous populations, as European powers sought to extract resources and impose their dominance over the land.

In modern times, El Dorado has transcended its origins to become a cultural symbol, representing not only the lure of wealth but also the folly of greed and the consequences of colonialism. The myth has been depicted in literature, art, and film, continuing to capture the imagination of people worldwide. It serves as a reminder of the complexities of human ambition, the destructive impacts of exploitation, and the enduring quest for prosperity that has shaped much of human history.

In conclusion, the legend of El Dorado is more than just a tale of a city made of gold; it is a reflection of humanity's perpetual pursuit of wealth and the moral questions that come with it. The myth has left a lasting impact on history, influencing exploration, colonialism, and our understanding of cultural exchanges between indigenous peoples and European colonizers. As we explore the enduring legacy of gold in human culture, the story of El Dorado remains a poignant example of how myths can shape our reality and aspirations.

The Philosopher's Stone: Alchemy and Gold

The quest for the Philosopher's Stone is one of the most enduring and fascinating narratives within the rich tapestry of alchemical history. Alchemy, a precursor to modern chemistry, was not merely a scientific endeavor but also a philosophical and spiritual journey that sought to transform not only materials but also the self. Central to this pursuit was the idea of transmutation—the ability to turn base metals, such as lead or mercury, into noble metals, primarily gold.

The Philosopher's Stone is often described as a mythical substance that could facilitate this extraordinary transformation. It was believed to possess the capability to convert base metals into gold and grant the secret of immortality through the Elixir of Life. While the Stone was considered a physical object, it also represented the alchemist's ultimate goal of achieving enlightenment and understanding the fundamental secrets of nature.

The origins of the Philosopher's Stone can be traced back to ancient civilizations, including Egypt and Greece, where the foundations of alchemical thought began to take shape. The Hermetic texts, attributed to Hermes Trismegistus—a syncretic figure combining the Greek god Hermes and the Egyptian god Thoth—served as critical sources of alchemical wisdom. These texts introduced the concept of "as above, so below," suggesting that the microcosm of human existence mirrored the macrocosm of the universe, thus linking the transformation of materials to spiritual enlightenment.

In medieval Europe, alchemy flourished, particularly during the 12th to 17th centuries. Alchemists such as Paracelsus, Nicolas Flamel, and John Dee contributed significantly to the lore surrounding the Philosopher's Stone. They embarked on extensive experiments, combining various substances and observing their reactions, all in hopes of uncovering the secrets of the Stone. The search for gold was not purely materialistic; it was intertwined with the quest for spiritual purity and perfection. The act of transmutation symbolized the alchemist's desire to elevate their soul from ignorance (represented by base metals) to enlightenment (symbolized by gold).

The allegorical nature of alchemical texts often obscured their true meanings, leading many to view them as mere recipes or magical incantations. However, the writings often contained profound philosophical insights, presenting the journey toward the Philosopher's Stone as a metaphor for personal transformation. The stages of alchemical processes—calcination, dissolution, separation, conjunction, fermentation, distillation, and coagulation—mirrored the inner journey of the alchemist, as they sought to purify and refine their own character.

Despite the incredible allure of the Philosopher's Stone, the scientific community eventually debunked many of the claims associated with alchemical practices. The emergence of modern chemistry, particularly in the 17th century, shifted the focus away from mystical pursuits toward empirical experimentation and the understanding of chemical reactions based on observable phenomena.

Nonetheless, the legacy of the Philosopher's Stone endures beyond its historical context. It has inspired countless literary and artistic works, becoming a symbol of transformation and the search for knowledge. In contemporary culture, the idea of the Philosopher's Stone resonates with themes of self-improvement, personal growth, and the ambition to attain one's highest potential.

In summary, the quest for the Philosopher's Stone encapsulates the alchemical pursuit of turning base metals into gold, reflecting deeper philosophical inquiries about transformation and enlightenment. This mythical substance serves as a reminder of humanity's timeless fascination with the interplay between material wealth and spiritual fulfillment, highlighting the intricate relationship between science, philosophy, and the human experience.

Gold in Ancient Folklore: Tales of Wealth and Woe

Throughout history, gold has held an enchanting allure that transcends mere economic value; it embodies dreams of wealth, power, and immortality. This precious metal has permeated folklore and fairy tales across cultures, often serving as a symbol of both prosperity and peril. The narratives surrounding gold reveal deep-seated human desires and fears, reflecting our complex relationship with this lustrous element.

One of the most famous tales involving gold is the legend of El Dorado, the fabled city of gold that drove countless explorers to the treacherous jungles of South America. Initially, the myth began with the account of a chieftain who covered himself in gold dust as a ritual offering to the gods. This account morphed into the story of an entire city glimmering with gold, leading to an era of relentless exploration fueled by greed and ambition. However, the pursuit of El Dorado often ended in tragedy and despair, as adventurers faced harsh realities—disease, hostile tribes, and the unforgiving terrain. The tale serves as a cautionary reminder of the folly of unbridled greed and the human cost of insatiable desire.

Gold's presence in folklore is not solely linked to wealth; it often conveys moral lessons about the consequences of avarice. In the Brothers Grimm fairy tale "Rumpelstiltskin," a miller boasts that his daughter can spin straw into gold, a claim that attracts the attention of a mysterious creature who demands her firstborn child in return for his magical assistance. This story encapsulates the idea that the pursuit of wealth can lead to dire consequences, emphasizing that the allure of gold can entrap individuals in moral dilemmas and personal sacrifices.

Similarly, in the tale of King Midas from Greek mythology, the king is granted the ability to turn everything he touches into gold. Initially, this gift seems like a blessing, allowing him to amass wealth beyond imagination. However, the curse reveals itself when Midas realizes that he cannot eat or drink, as even his food and water transform into gold. Midas's story serves as a poignant commentary on the pitfalls of greed—what is initially perceived as a boon becomes a source of suffering. The moral lesson is clear: the relentless pursuit of wealth can lead to isolation and despair, a theme that resonates through various cultures.

The concept of cursed gold appears in numerous folktales, reinforcing the idea that wealth can bring misfortune. The tale of King Solomon and the "Cursed Gold" reflects this belief, where treasures gained through deceit and treachery bring about the downfall of those who possess them. In many cultures, gold is seen as tempting yet dangerous, often associated with greed that leads to moral corruption and societal decay.

Moreover, gold is also depicted as a symbol of divine favor or punishment in various myths. In many traditions, the gods bestow gold as a sign of blessing upon the righteous, while it serves as a tool of punishment for those who stray from moral paths. This duality of gold—representing both the height of human aspiration and the depths of human folly—can be seen in tales from cultures around the globe, illustrating how gold's significance extends beyond material wealth.

In conclusion, the tales of gold in ancient folklore reflect humanity's enduring fascination with this precious metal. From the seductive promise of wealth to the cautionary tales of greed and its consequences, gold serves as a powerful symbol that encapsulates the complexities of human desire. As we navigate the contemporary world, these narratives remain relevant, reminding us of the timeless allure of gold and the lessons hidden within its gleaming surface.

The Curse of the Pharaohs: The Dark Side of Gold

Throughout history, gold has been revered as a symbol of wealth, power, and divinity, especially in ancient Egypt, where it was intricately linked to the concept of immortality and the afterlife. The allure of gold, however, has also given rise to a darker narrative—the so-called "Curse of the Pharaohs." This phenomenon intertwines the opulence of gold with tales of vengeance, retribution, and the supernatural, reflecting the belief systems and cultural perceptions of ancient Egyptians regarding death and the afterlife.

The legend of the Curse of the Pharaohs gained significant traction following the discovery of King Tutankhamun's tomb in 1922 by British archaeologist Howard Carter. The tomb, filled with exquisite gold artifacts, jewelry, and the famous golden mask, signified the immense wealth and resources that were buried along with the young pharaoh. However, the subsequent deaths of several individuals associated with the excavation sparked public fascination and fear. Among those who died were Lord Carnarvon, the expedition's financial backer, who succumbed to an infected mosquito bite, and several others who experienced untimely deaths or illnesses. This led to sensationalist media reports and the popular notion that a curse had been unleashed—a punishment for disturbing the eternal rest of the pharaoh.

The concept of curses in ancient Egyptian culture was not merely a product of superstition but was deeply rooted in their beliefs about the afterlife. Egyptians believed that the physical body was essential for the soul's journey into the afterlife, and thus, the tombs were filled with treasures, including gold, to assist the deceased in their journey. The protection of these tombs was paramount, and any disturbance could invoke the wrath of the gods, as well as the fury of the deceased. Hieroglyphics and inscriptions within tombs often contained warnings against intruders, suggesting that those who dared to violate the sanctity of the resting place would face dire consequences.

The allure of gold also contributed to the narratives surrounding curses. Gold was not only a material symbol of wealth but also represented divine favor. The ancient Egyptians believed that the gods bestowed both fortune and wrath through gold, and thus, the treasures buried with the pharaohs were seen as both a blessing and a potential source of danger. For instance, the gold artifacts found in tombs were often inscribed with prayers and spells intended to protect the deceased, but they were also perceived as triggers for curses against those who would defile sacred spaces.

As the legend of the Curse of the Pharaohs evolved, it became intertwined with broader themes of colonial exploitation and cultural misunderstanding. The Western fascination with Egyptology during the late 19th and early 20th centuries often romanticized and sensationalized ancient Egyptian culture, leading to a view of curses as a means of cultural resistance against foreign invaders. This notion was further popularized in literature and film, transforming the narrative of the curse into a compelling tale of adventure and intrigue.

In conclusion, the Curse of the Pharaohs encapsulates the rich tapestry of ancient Egyptian beliefs surrounding death and the afterlife, where gold played a pivotal role. While many of the tales associated with the curse may be exaggerated or unfounded, they reflect the profound respect and fear that ancient Egyptians held for their dead and the treasures that accompanied them. As modern interest in ancient Egypt continues, the allure of gold remains a potent symbol of both beauty and danger, reminding us of the complex interplay between wealth, power, and the human psyche.

Modern Myths: Gold Heists and Lost Treasures

Gold has fascinated humanity for millennia, not only as a symbol of wealth and power but also as the centerpiece of countless stories steeped in mystery and adventure. In the modern era, tales of gold heists and lost treasures continue to captivate public imagination, often blurring the lines between reality and fiction. These stories are fueled by the intrinsic allure of gold itself, which represents not just monetary value but also the dreams and aspirations associated with it.

The phenomenon of gold heists is particularly intriguing, as they often involve elaborate schemes, high-stakes planning, and, in some cases, breathtaking audacity. One of the most notorious examples is the 1983 Brink's-Mat heist at Heathrow Airport in London, where thieves made off with £26 million in gold bullion, diamonds, and cash. The heist was not only remarkable for the sheer scale of the theft but also for the subsequent fallout, which involved organized crime, betrayal, and even murder. The legend of this heist has evolved into a modern myth, inspiring books, documentaries, and films, all of which explore the dark allure of wealth obtained through crime.

Similarly, tales of lost treasures add to the mystique surrounding gold. The legend of the "Lost Dutchman's Gold Mine" in Arizona is one such story that has intrigued treasure hunters for decades. According to folklore, the mine is said to be filled with untold riches, but its exact location remains a mystery. Many adventurers have ventured into the Superstition Mountains, inspired by the promise of gold, yet few have returned with anything more than tales of hardship and danger. This narrative not only showcases the quest for gold but also underscores the human tendency to chase after dreams, often at great personal cost.

Moreover, the allure of gold has led to numerous stories of hidden treasures from shipwrecks and sunken galleons. The Spanish galleon Nuestra Señora de Atocha, which sank off the Florida Keys in 1622, became emblematic of lost treasures. It carried an estimated $400 million worth of gold and silver, and its discovery in the 1980s by treasure hunter Mel Fisher sparked a gold rush of sorts among treasure seekers. The tale of the Atocha not only highlights the risks associated with treasure hunting but also emphasizes the romantic idea of uncovering lost riches from the depths of history.

In popular culture, these myths and legends have inspired countless works of fiction, from novels to blockbuster films, often portraying treasure hunting as a thrilling adventure filled with danger and intrigue. The idea of a map leading to buried treasure or a secret society guarding ancient riches resonates deeply with audiences, reflecting a collective yearning for adventure and discovery. Films such as "Indiana Jones" and "National Treasure" tap into this archetype, revitalizing interest in historical mysteries and the quest for gold.

The modern myths surrounding gold heists and lost treasures serve as more than mere entertainment; they reflect societal values and anxieties about wealth, greed, and the pursuit of happiness. As gold continues to be a coveted asset, these stories remind us of the lengths to which individuals will go in their quest for riches, often leading to moral dilemmas and unforeseen consequences. In a world where wealth can shift rapidly, the allure of gold remains a powerful motivator, inspiring tales that echo through time, keeping the myths of gold alive and vibrant in contemporary culture.

Chapter 17

The Future of Gold Exploration

The Search for New Gold Deposits

Gold has captivated humanity for millennia, not just for its beauty but also for its economic value and cultural significance. As existing gold mines deplete and the demand for gold remains strong, the quest for new gold deposits has intensified. This search involves a combination of geological exploration, technological advancements, and the understanding of historical gold production regions.

Geological Exploration Techniques

The search for new gold deposits begins with geological exploration, which utilizes various techniques to locate areas rich in mineralization. Geologists study geological formations, rock types, and structural geology to identify regions that have the potential to host gold deposits. Techniques such as remote sensing, geophysical surveys, and geochemical analysis are employed to gather data about the earth's crust.

Remote sensing, for example, allows for the analysis of large areas of land from aerial or satellite imagery, helping to identify alterations in vegetation patterns and soil composition that may indicate the presence of gold. Geophysical surveys, including methods like magnetic and electromagnetic surveys, can detect anomalies in the Earth's magnetic field or electrical conductivity that suggest mineral deposits.

Historical Context: Proven Gold Regions

While new exploration technologies are promising, historical data remains invaluable in the search for new gold. Many significant gold deposits have been discovered in regions with a rich history of gold mining, such as the Witwatersrand Basin in South Africa, the Carlin Trend in Nevada, and the goldfields of Australia and Canada. These areas have been mined for decades, yet advancements in extraction methods and a deeper understanding of geology may reveal untapped resources.

For instance, the Carlin Trend, which has produced over 87 million ounces of gold since the 1960s, continues to hold potential for new discoveries. As companies refine their exploration techniques, they are discovering previously overlooked deposits in areas adjacent to historically productive zones.

Innovations in Technology
Technological advancements play a crucial role in the search for new gold deposits. Innovations in drilling techniques, such as diamond core drilling, allow for more precise sampling of geological formations, enabling geologists to identify the presence of gold at greater depths and in more challenging terrains. Additionally, the use of artificial intelligence (AI) and machine learning has transformed exploration strategies. These technologies analyze vast datasets to predict where gold deposits are likely to be found based on historical trends and geological patterns.

Furthermore, advancements in 3D modeling and visualization tools enable geologists to create detailed representations of subsurface geology, enhancing their ability to make informed decisions about where to conduct exploratory drilling.

Untapped Regions and Future Prospects
As the demand for gold increases, explorers are turning their attention to underexplored regions of the world. Emerging markets in Africa, South America, and even parts of Asia are gaining interest due to their geological potential and relatively low levels of exploration. For example, countries like Ethiopia and Ghana are becoming hotspots for gold exploration, with geological surveys indicating significant gold reserves that have yet to be fully tapped.

Additionally, the idea of deep-sea mining is beginning to take shape, with research suggesting that ocean floors may contain substantial gold deposits alongside other valuable minerals. While this approach raises environmental concerns, it could hold the key to discovering new gold sources in the future.

Conclusion
The search for new gold deposits is a dynamic and evolving field that combines traditional geological exploration with modern technology and innovative practices. As old mines are exhausted, the industry's focus shifts toward underexplored regions and the application of cutting-edge technologies. With the potential for significant discoveries still on the horizon, the quest for gold continues to be a driving force in the global economy, shaping the future of this precious metal and the industries that rely on it.

Technological Advances in Gold Prospecting
The quest for gold has been a defining part of human history, influencing economies, cultures, and even geopolitical landscapes. As demand for gold continues to rise, so does the need for more efficient, sustainable, and innovative methods of exploration and extraction. Technological advances are at the forefront of revolutionizing gold prospecting, merging traditional methods

with cutting-edge innovations to enhance the efficacy of locating and extracting this precious metal.

Remote Sensing and Geophysical Methods

One of the most significant advancements in gold prospecting is the use of remote sensing technologies. Satellite imagery and aerial surveys have become invaluable tools for geologists. These technologies allow for the analysis of vast areas of land without the need for extensive ground surveys. By employing multispectral and hyperspectral imaging, geologists can identify mineralogical signatures and anomalies associated with gold deposits. In particular, these methods can highlight areas with altered rock types, which often signify the presence of gold-bearing veins.

In addition to remote sensing, geophysical techniques such as magnetic, electrical, and seismic surveys provide critical information about subsurface geology. These non-invasive methods can reveal the structure and composition of the Earth's crust, helping prospectors identify promising sites for further exploration. For instance, induced polarization (IP) surveys can detect the presence of disseminated gold in sulfide minerals, guiding drill sites more precisely.

Geological Modelling and Data Analytics

The integration of advanced data analytics and geological modelling software has transformed how geologists interpret exploration data. Geographic Information Systems (GIS) allow for the layering of various data types—geological, geochemical, and geophysical—enabling a comprehensive analysis of potential gold deposits. These models can simulate geological processes and visualize the spatial relationships between mineralization and geological features.

Moreover, machine learning algorithms are increasingly being employed to analyze vast datasets generated from exploration activities. By identifying patterns and correlations within these datasets, machine learning can help predict where undiscovered gold deposits might be located. This predictive capability significantly reduces the time and cost of exploration, allowing for a more focused and systematic approach in identifying viable mining sites.

Innovations in Drilling Technology

The traditional methods of drilling for gold have also seen substantial improvements. Modern drilling technologies, such as diamond core drilling and reverse circulation drilling, provide more accurate and efficient means of obtaining rock samples. These methods allow for faster and deeper drilling while minimizing environmental impact. Additionally, advancements in drilling rigs equipped with automated systems enhance precision and safety, reducing the risk associated with manual drilling operations.

Furthermore, the introduction of remotely operated vehicles (ROVs) and drones is revolutionizing how exploration teams conduct fieldwork. Drones equipped with high-resolution cameras and sensors can quickly survey large areas, capturing data that was once time-consuming and labor-intensive to collect. This capability not only speeds up the exploration process but also enables teams to access challenging terrains that would be difficult for traditional machinery.

Sustainable Practices and Environmental Considerations
As technology advances, so does the emphasis on sustainable practices in gold prospecting. Innovations in exploration techniques focus on minimizing ecological footprints through reduced land disturbance and precise targeting of mineral deposits. Technologies such as biodegradable drilling fluids and environmentally friendly geochemical methods are being developed to lessen the environmental impact associated with traditional gold mining practices.

In conclusion, technological advances in gold prospecting are fundamentally reshaping the landscape of gold exploration. From remote sensing and geophysical methods to sophisticated data analytics and innovative drilling technologies, these developments not only enhance the efficiency of finding gold but also promote more sustainable and environmentally conscious practices. As the demand for gold continues to evolve, so too will the methods used to uncover its hidden treasures, paving the way for a more responsible and effective gold mining industry.

The Role of Artificial Intelligence in Gold Mining
The integration of Artificial Intelligence (AI) into the gold mining industry marks a significant technological advancement that has the potential to revolutionize how gold is located, extracted, and processed. As the demand for gold continues to rise in various sectors, including jewelry, electronics, and investment, the need for efficient and sustainable mining practices has become increasingly critical. AI technologies are emerging as pivotal tools in achieving these goals, enhancing both productivity and environmental stewardship.

Locating Gold Deposits
One of the foremost applications of AI in gold mining is in the exploration phase, where the challenge lies in identifying potential gold deposits. Traditional exploration methods can be labor-intensive and costly, often requiring extensive geological surveys and drilling. AI can streamline this process by utilizing machine learning algorithms to analyze vast datasets, including geological, geochemical, and geophysical information.

These algorithms can identify patterns and correlations that human geologists might overlook, leading to the identification of promising exploration sites. For example, AI can process satellite imagery and geospatial data to pinpoint areas with a higher probability of gold presence, thereby significantly reducing the time and cost associated with exploration.

Enhancing Extraction Techniques

Once gold deposits are located, the extraction process can also benefit from AI technologies. Advanced AI systems can optimize the mining operations by predicting the most efficient methods to extract gold while minimizing waste and reducing environmental impact. By analyzing data from previous mining activities, AI can provide insights into the best practices for drilling, blasting, and haulage.

Moreover, AI-driven predictive maintenance can improve the reliability of mining equipment. By continuously monitoring machinery performance and predicting failures before they occur, mining companies can reduce downtime and maintenance costs, thus enhancing overall operational efficiency.

Processing and Refining Gold

AI is not only transforming the exploration and extraction processes but is also playing a crucial role in the processing and refining stages of gold mining. The refining process often involves complex chemical reactions to separate gold from other materials. AI algorithms can optimize these processes by analyzing the composition of the ore in real time, adjusting the refining parameters to maximize yield and minimize the use of hazardous chemicals.

Furthermore, AI can also assist in monitoring environmental parameters during processing. By analyzing data from sensors placed throughout the processing plant, AI systems can ensure compliance with environmental regulations, thereby reducing the ecological footprint of gold mining operations.

Sustainability and Environmental Monitoring

The environmental impact of gold mining has come under increased scrutiny, prompting the industry to adopt more sustainable practices. AI technology can help in this regard by monitoring environmental conditions around mining sites. For instance, AI can analyze data related to water quality, soil conditions, and biodiversity, allowing companies to make informed decisions that minimize environmental harm.

Additionally, AI can support the reclamation of mined lands by identifying the best techniques for restoring ecosystems after mining operations have ceased. The use of AI in these contexts not only helps companies adhere to environmental regulations but also enhances their corporate social responsibility initiatives.

Conclusion

The role of Artificial Intelligence in gold mining is multifaceted, offering solutions that enhance exploration, extraction, processing, and sustainability. As AI technologies continue to evolve, their integration into the gold mining sector will likely grow, leading to more efficient operations and reduced environmental impacts. The future of gold mining may very well hinge on the successful application of these advanced technologies, ensuring that the industry can meet the growing demand for gold in a responsible manner. Through AI, the gold mining sector is poised to become more innovative, sustainable, and adaptable in the face of global challenges.

Gold from Space: Asteroid Mining and Beyond

The exploration of outer space has ignited humanity's imagination for centuries, and with the advent of advanced technologies, the prospect of mining celestial bodies, particularly asteroids, has become a tangible reality. This potential for extracting valuable resources, including gold, from space presents both exciting opportunities and complex challenges.

Asteroids are remnants from the early solar system, composed of various minerals and metals, including precious metals such as gold, platinum, and rare earth elements. Current estimates indicate that some of these asteroids contain more metal than exists on Earth, leading scientists and entrepreneurs to explore the feasibility of asteroid mining as a new frontier for resource extraction.

One of the most attractive aspects of asteroid mining is the abundance of resources that could be harvested. For instance, it is estimated that a single asteroid, like 16 Psyche, which is believed to be composed largely of metallic iron and nickel, might contain resources worth hundreds of billions of dollars. This asteroid, located in the asteroid belt between Mars and Jupiter, is just one of many that could potentially provide a wealth of metals, including gold. The allure of such wealth has fueled interest from private companies, governments, and researchers alike.

The technology to identify and reach these asteroids is advancing rapidly. Probes and space missions, such as NASA's OSIRIS-REx and Japan's Hayabusa2, have successfully visited asteroids to gather data and samples. These missions not only enhance our understanding of asteroids but also pave the way for future manned missions aimed at mining operations. As rocket technology continues to improve, the cost of sending missions to asteroids is expected to decrease, making it more economically viable to extract materials from space.

However, the challenges of asteroid mining are significant. The technical difficulties of landing on and extracting materials from an asteroid are immense. Spacecraft must be equipped with specialized tools to mine the asteroids, and these operations would need to be automated due to the distance from Earth and the harsh conditions of space. Moreover, the logistics of transporting mined materials back to Earth pose additional challenges. Current propulsion technologies would require considerable advancements to make such missions feasible and cost-effective.

Legal and regulatory issues also complicate asteroid mining. The Outer Space Treaty of 1967, signed by over 100 countries, including major spacefaring nations, states that celestial bodies cannot be claimed by any one nation. This presents a dilemma regarding the ownership of resources extracted from asteroids. As the technology develops, there will be a need for international agreements to govern the rights to mine and profit from space resources.

Despite these challenges, the potential benefits of asteroid mining are compelling. Beyond gold and other precious metals, asteroids could provide essential materials for space exploration and colonization, such as water, which can be converted into hydrogen and oxygen for fuel. This capability could lead to sustainable practices in space travel and help establish permanent human presence beyond Earth.

In conclusion, the prospect of mining gold and other valuable resources from asteroids represents a bold new frontier in both space exploration and resource management. While the technical, legal, and logistical hurdles are substantial, the ongoing advancements in space technology and the growing interest from various sectors suggest that the dream of asteroid mining may become a reality in the not-so-distant future. As humanity looks to the stars, the allure of gold from space captures not only the imagination but also the potential for a new era of resource utilization beyond our planet.

Sustainable Gold Mining: The Next Frontier

As the global demand for gold continues to rise, the mining industry faces increasing scrutiny over its environmental impact. Traditionally, gold mining has been associated with significant ecological degradation—deforestation, soil erosion, water pollution, and disruption of local ecosystems. However, a shift towards sustainable gold mining practices is emerging as the industry seeks to balance profitability with environmental stewardship. This transformation is not merely a response to ethical considerations; it also recognizes the long-term viability of mining operations in a world increasingly focused on sustainability.

The Imperative for Sustainable Practices

The mining sector is at a crossroads. With climate change and biodiversity loss becoming pressing global challenges, there is an urgent need to adopt practices that minimize harm to the environment. Sustainable gold mining aims to reduce the ecological footprint of gold extraction by implementing innovative techniques and technologies. This includes the use of eco-friendly extraction methods, responsible waste management, and rehabilitation of mined sites.

Technological Innovations

Recent advancements in technology are playing a crucial role in promoting sustainable gold mining. For example, the use of cyanide-free processes for gold extraction is gaining traction. These methods, which utilize less toxic alternatives, significantly reduce the risk of soil and water contamination. Additionally, innovations in mineral processing, such as bioleaching—where microorganisms are used to extract metals from ores—present a promising avenue for reducing the environmental impact of mining.

Moreover, the integration of renewable energy sources into mining operations is crucial for reducing carbon emissions. Solar and wind power can help diminish the reliance on fossil fuels, making operations more sustainable. Companies are increasingly investing in renewable energy projects to power mining sites, which can significantly lower their carbon footprint.

Community Engagement and Ethical Practices

Sustainable gold mining also emphasizes the importance of engaging local communities and respecting indigenous rights. Community-led initiatives can lead to more responsible mining practices that prioritize the welfare of local populations. By involving communities in decision-making processes and offering them a stake in mining operations, companies can foster goodwill and reduce conflicts. This approach not only benefits the community but also enhances the social license to operate, which is crucial for the long-term success of mining projects.

Ethical sourcing of gold is another critical aspect of sustainable mining. With the rise of consumer awareness regarding the origins of products, more companies are committing to ensuring that their gold is sourced responsibly. Initiatives like the Responsible Gold Mining Principles (RGMPs) and the OECD Due Diligence Guidance for Responsible Supply Chains are setting standards for ethical sourcing in the industry. These frameworks guide miners in adopting practices that mitigate negative impacts on the environment and local communities.

The Role of Regulation and Certification

Regulatory frameworks are essential for promoting sustainable mining practices. Governments and international organizations are beginning to implement stricter regulations regarding environmental protection, waste management, and labor rights within the mining sector. Certification programs can also play a pivotal role by providing assurance to consumers that the gold they purchase is produced sustainably. These certifications increase transparency and encourage companies to adhere to high environmental and ethical standards.

A Forward-Looking Perspective
As the industry moves towards sustainable gold mining, it is crucial for stakeholders—miners, governments, investors, and consumers—to collaborate. By fostering partnerships and sharing best practices, the mining sector can evolve to meet the demands of a modern, sustainability-focused economy. The transition to sustainable practices not only addresses environmental concerns but also positions gold mining as a responsible and forward-thinking industry.

In conclusion, the future of gold mining lies in its ability to reconcile profit with environmental stewardship. By embracing technological innovations, engaging communities, adhering to ethical standards, and supporting regulatory frameworks, the gold mining sector can pave the way for a more sustainable and responsible future. This shift not only benefits the planet but also ensures the longevity and profitability of gold mining in an increasingly conscientious world.

Chapter 18

Gold in Global Trade and Economics

Gold as a Global Commodity: Trade and Exchange

Gold has held a unique position in the global economy for centuries, serving not only as a symbol of wealth and status but also as a fundamental commodity that underpins financial systems and trade practices worldwide. Its intrinsic properties—scarcity, durability, and divisibility—make gold a highly desirable asset, leading to its continuous demand in various sectors including jewelry, technology, and investment.

The Structure of Gold Trading

Gold trading occurs in both physical and paper forms. The most common venues for physical gold trading include exchanges such as the London Bullion Market and the Shanghai Gold Exchange. The London Bullion Market is particularly significant, as it acts as a benchmark for gold pricing globally. Here, gold is traded in large quantities, with transactions often conducted over the phone or through electronic systems. The price of gold is determined by the spot market, influenced by factors such as supply and demand dynamics, geopolitical events, currency fluctuations, and economic indicators.

In addition to physical trading, gold is also traded in paper form through futures contracts and exchange-traded funds (ETFs). Futures contracts allow investors to buy or sell gold at a predetermined price at a future date, providing a hedge against price fluctuations. ETFs, on the other hand, offer investors an opportunity to gain exposure to gold without the need to hold the physical metal. These financial instruments have democratized access to gold investment, making it easier for both retail and institutional investors to participate in gold markets.

Global Demand for Gold

Globally, the demand for gold is driven by several key sectors. Jewelry remains the largest consumer of gold, particularly in countries like India and China, where cultural traditions and festivals drive significant jewelry purchases. The demand for gold in technology is also noteworthy; gold's excellent conductivity and resistance to corrosion make it essential in electronics, from smartphones to computers. Furthermore, gold is often viewed as a safe-haven asset during times of economic uncertainty, which can lead to spikes in investment demand.

Central banks around the world also play a critical role in gold trading. Many central banks hold gold reserves as part of their monetary policy strategy, buying and selling gold to manage currency values and stabilize their economies. In recent years, several countries have increased their gold purchases, reflecting a growing trend of diversifying reserves away from traditional fiat currencies.

The Role of Gold in International Trade
Gold functions as a universal medium of exchange, often used in international trade to settle debts or transactions, especially in regions with unstable currencies. The liquidity of gold means that it can be easily converted into cash or used in trade agreements, making it a vital asset in global commerce. Countries with significant gold reserves have a greater bargaining power in international negotiations, as gold can serve as collateral or a means of securing trade deals.

Price Influences and Market Dynamics
The price of gold is influenced by a complex interplay of factors, including inflation rates, interest rates, and geopolitical tensions. For instance, during periods of high inflation, investors flock to gold as a hedge, driving up its price. Conversely, rising interest rates can make other investments more attractive, leading to decreased demand for gold.

Moreover, the emergence of digital currencies and financial technologies poses new challenges and opportunities for gold trading. As cryptocurrencies gain traction, they may change how investors perceive gold's role as a store of value, leading to shifts in trading patterns.

Conclusion
In conclusion, gold's status as a global commodity is firmly entrenched in the fabric of international trade and finance. Its unique attributes, combined with the diverse demand across various sectors, ensure that gold will continue to be a pivotal asset in global markets. As economic landscapes evolve, the mechanisms of gold trading will also adapt, cementing gold's legacy as a timeless and essential commodity in the global economy.

The Impact of Gold on National Economies
Gold has historically held a pivotal role in shaping national economies, serving as a cornerstone of monetary systems and a symbol of wealth and stability. Its influence manifests in various dimensions, including currency stability, trade balances, investment attractiveness, and economic policy formulation.

Currency Stability and the Gold Standard

For centuries, many nations operated under the gold standard, a monetary system in which the value of a country's currency was directly linked to a specific amount of gold. This linkage provided a stable and predictable currency value, fostering trust among investors and consumers. Countries adhering to this standard experienced reduced inflation rates and greater economic stability, as the supply of money was limited by the availability of gold reserves. However, the gold standard also imposed constraints on monetary policy. Governments could not easily adjust money supply in response to economic fluctuations, which sometimes led to deflationary pressures during economic downturns.

The shift away from the gold standard in the 20th century prompted significant changes in how nations managed their economies. While fiat currencies provided greater flexibility for governments to respond to economic crises, the absence of a tangible asset backing currency raised concerns about inflation and currency devaluation. Nevertheless, the legacy of the gold standard continues to influence contemporary monetary policies and serves as a benchmark for countries seeking to establish credibility in their currency.

Trade Balances and Gold Reserves

Gold production and reserves directly impact a nation's trade balance. Countries rich in gold resources can benefit economically from exports; for example, gold mining can lead to substantial revenues and foreign exchange earnings, enhancing the national economy. These nations often experience a favorable trade balance, as gold exports can offset imports, contributing to a positive current account.

Moreover, gold reserves held by central banks act as a financial safety net for nations. During times of geopolitical instability or economic uncertainty, countries with substantial gold reserves can rely on these assets to stabilize their currencies and reduce volatility in financial markets. Additionally, gold reserves enhance international credibility, as countries with significant reserves are often viewed as more stable and trustworthy by global investors.

Investment Attractiveness

The presence of gold resources can significantly influence national investment climates. Countries with abundant gold deposits attract both domestic and foreign investments in mining and related industries. These investments can stimulate economic growth by creating jobs, fostering local businesses, and generating tax revenues for governments. Moreover, a thriving gold mining sector can lead to the development of infrastructure, such as roads, energy supplies, and communication systems, benefiting the broader economy.

Conversely, countries with limited gold resources may find themselves at a disadvantage. Without significant natural resources, these nations may struggle to attract investment or achieve economic diversification, making them vulnerable to external shocks and fluctuations in commodity prices.

Economic Policy Formulation

Gold's importance in national economies also influences government policies. Countries rich in gold may prioritize resource management and sustainability, ensuring that mining activities do not lead to environmental degradation or social unrest. Moreover, the revenues generated from gold production can be directed toward infrastructure projects, education, and healthcare, promoting long-term economic development.

In contrast, nations reliant on gold mining may face challenges, including the "resource curse," where an overreliance on a single commodity leads to economic instability, corruption, and neglect of other sectors. This phenomenon highlights the need for balanced economic policies that promote diversification and sustainable growth.

Conclusion

In conclusion, gold's impact on national economies is profound and multifaceted. From serving as a foundation for monetary stability to influencing trade balances and investment attractiveness, gold continues to shape economic policies and national fortunes. As the global economy evolves, the role of gold may transition, but its historical significance ensures that it remains a critical component of economic discourse and strategy. Understanding the dynamics of gold production and reserves will be essential for nations aiming to harness its potential for sustainable economic growth.

Gold and International Relations: A Historical Perspective

Gold has been a pivotal element in shaping international relations throughout history, serving not just as a medium of exchange but as a symbol of power, wealth, and prestige. The allure of gold can be traced back to ancient civilizations, where it played a crucial role in diplomacy, trade, and conflict. The historical trajectory of gold reveals how it has influenced diplomatic relations, shaped alliances, and even incited wars.

In ancient times, gold was often used to facilitate trade between nations. Merchants and diplomats carried gold as a trusted currency that could be exchanged for goods and services. Civilizations such as the Egyptians, Mesopotamians, and Indus Valley peoples utilized gold not only in their domestic economies but also as a means to establish and enhance trade relations with neighboring cultures. The desire for gold was a significant driver of exploration, as seen during the Age of Exploration when European powers sought new trade routes to access gold-rich territories.

The connection between gold and diplomacy became particularly evident during the Roman Empire. Gold coins were not merely currency; they were also a tool of political power. The denarius, a silver coin that often had a gold equivalent in terms of value, was used to pay soldiers, fund construction projects, and solidify alliances. Roman emperors would often distribute gold coins to win favor among the populace and foreign dignitaries, thereby strengthening their diplomatic ties.

In the Middle Ages, gold continued to play a significant role in diplomacy. European monarchs used gold as a diplomatic tool to secure alliances through marriage and treaties. The lavish gifts of gold and precious metals were often exchanged between royal families, symbolizing both wealth and goodwill. The Byzantine Empire, with its rich gold traditions, utilized gold to maintain its influence and negotiate with neighboring states.

The Islamic Golden Age saw a flourishing of trade routes that interconnected Europe, Asia, and Africa, with gold being a crucial commodity. The establishment of the Islamic caliphates allowed for the unification of various regions under a shared economic framework that relied heavily on gold. Diplomatic relations were often solidified through the exchange of gold, which served as a common language of value and trust.

As the modern era dawned, gold took on new dimensions in international relations. The establishment of the gold standard in the 19th century transformed monetary systems globally, influencing trade policies and diplomatic negotiations. Nations sought to accumulate gold reserves to bolster their economic standing, leading to competitive relationships based on gold holdings. The scramble for colonies and resources during the colonial period was often driven by the pursuit of gold, leading to conflicts and realignments that shaped modern nation-states.

In the 20th century, the role of gold in international relations evolved further with the Bretton Woods Agreement, which established a system of fixed exchange rates tied to gold. This framework aimed to create stability in global trade and foster cooperation among nations, illustrating how gold continued to act as a linchpin in diplomatic relations.

Today, while the direct influence of gold on diplomatic relations may have waned with the advent of fiat currencies and digital assets, its historical significance remains evident. Gold's enduring legacy as a symbol of wealth, power, and trust continues to resonate in international relations, particularly in times of economic uncertainty. Nations still view gold reserves as a safeguard against financial crises, reinforcing its role as a strategic asset in global diplomacy.

In summary, gold has profoundly influenced the course of international relations throughout history. From facilitating trade and securing alliances to shaping economic policies and diplomatic strategies, gold's allure and intrinsic value have made it a cornerstone of human interaction on the global stage. Its role in diplomacy underscores the complex interplay between wealth, power, and international relations, a dynamic that remains relevant even in contemporary discussions surrounding economic policy and global governance.

The Role of Gold in Modern Economic Crises

Gold has long held a reputation as a safe haven asset, particularly during periods of economic uncertainty and turmoil. This status is deeply rooted in both its physical properties and its historical context. Unlike paper currency, which can be subject to inflation and devaluation, gold has intrinsic value due to its scarcity, durability, and universal acceptance. During economic crises, when confidence in financial institutions and fiat currencies wanes, investors often turn to gold as a protective measure for their wealth.

Historically, during times of financial instability, gold prices have tended to rise as demand increases. For instance, during the 2008 financial crisis, gold reached record highs as investors sought security amidst collapsing stock markets and failing banks. The crisis was characterized by unprecedented government bailouts and quantitative easing measures that undermined trust in monetary systems. As central banks flooded economies with liquidity, fears of hyperinflation grew, prompting a rush to gold as a hedge against currency devaluation.

The COVID-19 pandemic further illustrated gold's role as a safe haven. As global economies faced lockdowns and severe economic contraction, governments implemented massive stimulus packages. Uncertainty regarding the recovery of economies led to heightened fears of inflation and currency instability. In this environment, gold prices surged, reaching an all-time high in August 2020. Investors flocked to gold not only for its historical stability but also for its potential to preserve value in an unpredictable market.

Moreover, gold's appeal during economic downturns is influenced by its historical significance as a store of value. For centuries, gold has been associated with wealth and power, making it a trusted asset in times of crisis. This perception is reinforced by the fact that central banks around the world hold substantial gold reserves as part of their monetary policy. These reserves serve as a buffer against economic shocks, lending further credibility to gold as a reliable asset during turbulent times.

The rise of financial instruments such as gold exchange-traded funds (ETFs) has also democratized access to gold investment. Investors no longer need to physically purchase and store gold; they can buy shares in funds that hold gold bullion, making it easier to invest in this precious metal during uncertain times. This accessibility has contributed to gold's popularity as a safe haven asset among retail and institutional investors alike.

Despite its reputation as a safe haven, investing in gold is not without risks. While gold can provide protection against inflation and currency depreciation, its prices can be volatile in the short term. Factors such as changes in interest rates, geopolitical tensions, and shifts in global demand can all impact gold prices. Nevertheless, many investors view gold as a strategic component of a diversified portfolio, particularly during periods of economic stress.

In conclusion, gold's role as a safe haven during economic crises is a well-established phenomenon. Its intrinsic value, historical significance, and universal acceptance make it a preferred asset for investors seeking stability amid uncertainty. As global economies continue to grapple with challenges, from inflationary pressures to geopolitical tensions, gold is likely to remain a cornerstone of wealth preservation strategies, reinforcing its enduring legacy as a protective asset in the modern financial landscape.

The Future of Gold in the Global Economy

As we navigate the complexities of the 21st century, the role of gold in the global economy continues to evolve, shaped by technological advancements, geopolitical shifts, and changing consumer behaviors. Historically viewed as a safe haven asset, gold has weathered economic storms, and its future seems poised to reflect both enduring traditions and modern innovations.

One of the most significant factors influencing gold's future is the ongoing debate surrounding monetary systems. The traditional gold standard, where currencies were directly tied to gold reserves, is largely a relic of the past. However, the increasing volatility in global financial markets has sparked discussions about returning to a system that incorporates gold as a stabilizing force. Advocates argue that gold can serve as a hedge against inflation and currency devaluation, particularly in times of economic uncertainty. As central banks around the world amass gold reserves, its potential return to a more prominent role in monetary policy may reshape global finance.

Furthermore, gold's intrinsic value is increasingly being recognized in the context of digital currencies. The rise of cryptocurrencies has led to comparisons between digital assets and gold, often referred to as "digital gold." While cryptocurrencies like Bitcoin offer decentralized alternatives to traditional currencies, gold retains a historical and cultural significance that digital currencies lack. The interplay between these two asset classes will likely shape investment strategies and economic policies in the years to come. For many investors, gold remains a tangible asset with a proven track record of preserving wealth, while digital currencies present a new frontier of speculative investment.

Technological advancements are also set to influence gold's future in profound ways. Innovations in mining and refining technologies have the potential to reduce costs and improve efficiency, making gold extraction more sustainable and environmentally friendly. The growing emphasis on ethical sourcing and responsible mining practices is likely to affect consumer preferences, with a shift towards gold that meets rigorous environmental and social standards. Companies that prioritize sustainability may find themselves at a competitive advantage as consumers become increasingly conscious of the ethical implications of their purchases.

The global trade dynamics surrounding gold are also changing. Emerging markets, particularly in Asia, are becoming significant players in the gold market. Countries like China and India not only consume vast quantities of gold but are also investing in their own mining operations, affecting global supply chains. This shift could lead to a more decentralized gold market, where price influences are not solely dictated by Western economies. As these economies continue to grow, their impact on gold demand will shape pricing dynamics and investment strategies across the globe.

Moreover, the environmental impact of gold mining is under intense scrutiny. As climate change becomes an increasingly urgent issue, the gold industry is being called upon to adopt more sustainable practices. Innovations in eco-friendly extraction methods and recycling initiatives are gaining traction, allowing for a more responsible approach to gold production. The future of gold mining may hinge on the industry's ability to balance profitability with environmental stewardship, ensuring that gold remains a valued commodity in a changing world.

The future of gold in the global economy is thus a tapestry woven from threads of tradition and innovation. While gold's historical significance as a store of value persists, its role may evolve amid technological advancements, geopolitical shifts, and an increasing demand for ethical practices. As investors, policymakers, and consumers navigate this landscape, gold will likely continue to be regarded not just as a financial asset but as a multifaceted symbol of wealth, security, and resilience in an ever-changing world.

Chapter 19

The Environmental Future of Gold

Addressing the Environmental Impact of Gold Mining

Gold mining has long been associated with significant environmental degradation, including deforestation, soil erosion, water contamination, and habitat destruction. As the demand for gold continues to rise, the industry faces mounting pressure to mitigate its ecological footprint. In recent years, various approaches and innovations have emerged, reflecting a growing awareness of the need for sustainable practices in gold extraction and processing.

The Rise of Sustainable Mining Practices

One of the most pressing environmental challenges posed by gold mining is the use of toxic chemicals, particularly cyanide and mercury, in the extraction process. These substances can leach into local water sources, affecting aquatic life and posing health risks to communities. In response, many mining companies are adopting alternative methods that minimize or eliminate the use of harmful chemicals. For instance, bioleaching—a process that utilizes bacteria to extract gold from ore—has gained traction as a more environmentally friendly technique. This method not only reduces chemical use but also lowers energy consumption, making it a more sustainable option.

Increased Regulation and Industry Standards

Governments and international organizations have begun to implement stricter regulations aimed at reducing the environmental impacts of gold mining. The International Council on Mining and Metals (ICMM) has developed a set of sustainable development principles that member companies are encouraged to adopt. These principles include commitments to environmental stewardship, community engagement, and transparency in operations. As part of this initiative, many companies are conducting environmental impact assessments (EIAs) before commencing mining activities to identify potential risks and develop mitigation strategies.

Moreover, some nations are enforcing stricter laws regarding land use and waste management in mining operations. For instance, the gradual phasing out of mercury in artisanal and small-scale gold mining (ASGM)—a significant source of mercury pollution—has become a priority in many countries. Initiatives such as the Minamata Convention on Mercury aim to reduce mercury use globally, promoting safer alternatives and supporting the transition to sustainable mining practices.

Innovations in Eco-Friendly Gold Extraction

Technological advancements have also played a crucial role in addressing environmental challenges in gold mining. Companies are increasingly investing in research and development to create eco-friendly extraction techniques. Innovations such as the use of non-toxic leaching agents, including thiosulfate and glycine, are being explored as alternatives to cyanide. These methods not only reduce the toxicity of mining operations but also demonstrate comparable efficiency in gold recovery.

Additionally, advancements in remote sensing and drone technology are enhancing the ability to monitor environmental impacts more effectively. These technologies allow for real-time assessments of land use changes, vegetation loss, and water quality, enabling mining companies to respond quickly to environmental concerns.

Community Engagement and Local Initiatives

Sustainable gold mining is not solely the responsibility of corporations; community engagement is essential for mitigating environmental impacts. Many mining companies are partnering with local communities to promote sustainable practices. This includes supporting community-led initiatives that focus on reforestation, soil conservation, and water quality improvement. By involving local stakeholders in decision-making processes, companies can foster a sense of ownership and responsibility towards the environment.

In some regions, artisanal miners are being provided with training and resources to adopt more sustainable methods. Programs aimed at educating miners about responsible practices and the risks associated with traditional gold extraction techniques are vital for reducing environmental harm.

Conclusion

While the environmental impact of gold mining remains a significant concern, the industry is increasingly recognizing its responsibility to adopt sustainable practices. Through the implementation of innovative technologies, adherence to stricter regulations, and active community engagement, the gold mining sector is taking steps toward reducing its ecological footprint. As the demand for gold continues to grow, these efforts will be critical in ensuring that mining can coexist with environmental stewardship, ultimately leading to a more sustainable future for both the industry and the planet.

Innovations in Eco-Friendly Gold Extraction

The gold mining industry has long been associated with environmental degradation, including habitat destruction, water pollution, and toxic chemical use. In response to these challenges, there has been a significant push towards innovations in eco-friendly gold extraction methods. These techniques not only aim to minimize the ecological footprint of mining operations but also enhance efficiency and sustainability.

1. Biomining: Harnessing Microorganisms

One of the most promising innovations in eco-friendly gold extraction is biomining, which employs microorganisms to extract precious metals from ores. Certain bacteria and archaea can naturally leach gold from ores through biochemical processes. For example, Thiobacillus ferrooxidans is a bacterium that oxidizes iron and sulfide minerals, releasing gold ions that can be collected. This method is considerably less harmful to the environment compared to traditional chemical processes, which often involve cyanide or mercury, both of which pose significant health risks and environmental hazards.

2. Thiosulfate Leaching

Thiosulfate leaching is an emerging alternative to cyanide leaching, which is the conventional method used for gold extraction. Thiosulfate is less toxic than cyanide and can be used to dissolve gold from ores. This technique has gained traction due to its lower environmental impact and its ability to extract gold from ores that are resistant to cyanide. Thiosulfate leaching can also reclaim gold from tailings—waste materials left after the extraction process—making it a dual-benefit technology that aids in waste management and resource recovery.

3. Gravity Separation Techniques

Gravity separation methods have been refined to enhance gold recovery while reducing environmental impact. Techniques such as spiral concentrators, shaking tables, and centrifugal concentrators exploit the difference in density between gold and other materials to separate gold from ore without the need for toxic chemicals. These methods are particularly beneficial for alluvial gold deposits and can be implemented in small-scale mining operations, promoting local economic development without overwhelming environmental costs.

4. Electrowinning and Membrane Technology

Electrowinning is a process that extracts metals from solutions using electric current. In the context of gold mining, it allows for the recovery of gold from leach solutions without the use of harmful chemicals. Innovations in membrane technology are also being researched to improve the efficiency of electrowinning processes, allowing for more selective separation of gold ions from other metals. This not only enhances recovery rates but also minimizes waste and energy consumption.

5. Closed-Loop Systems
The adoption of closed-loop systems in gold mining operations is essential for minimizing water usage and preventing contamination. These systems recycle water used in mining, which drastically reduces the demand for fresh water and limits the discharge of polluted water into local ecosystems. Closed-loop systems also enable the recovery and reuse of chemicals used in extraction, further reducing environmental impact.

6. Sustainable Practices and Community Engagement
Beyond technological innovations, the future of eco-friendly gold extraction heavily relies on sustainable practices and community engagement. Responsible mining companies are increasingly adopting practices that promote environmental stewardship, including reforestation initiatives, habitat restoration, and community-led monitoring programs. Engaging local communities in decision-making processes ensures that mining operations consider social and environmental priorities, fostering a shared sense of responsibility for the land.

Conclusion
Innovations in eco-friendly gold extraction represent a critical shift in the mining industry, moving towards practices that prioritize environmental health alongside economic viability. As technology continues to advance, the prospect of sustainable gold mining becomes more achievable, paving the way for a future where gold can be extracted with minimal harm to the planet and its inhabitants. These advancements not only address the pressing environmental concerns associated with gold extraction but also contribute to the long-term sustainability of the gold industry.

The Role of Governments in Regulating Gold Mining

Gold mining has long been a significant economic driver, contributing to national revenues, providing employment opportunities, and fostering technological advancements. However, the extraction of gold is not without its challenges, particularly in terms of environmental degradation, social impacts, and economic inequalities. Consequently, governments worldwide play a pivotal role in regulating gold mining, shaping the industry's future through policies, laws, and partnerships that balance economic interests with environmental and social responsibilities.

Legislative Frameworks and Licensing
At the core of governmental regulation is the establishment of legislative frameworks that govern gold mining activities. Governments typically require mining companies to obtain licenses before commencing exploration and extraction. These licenses often come with

stringent conditions aimed at ensuring compliance with environmental laws, labor regulations, and community engagement practices. For instance, many countries mandate Environmental Impact Assessments (EIAs) that assess the potential effects of mining on local ecosystems and communities before granting mining permits. This regulatory step not only safeguards the environment but also holds mining companies accountable for their operations.

In addition to EIAs, many governments impose specific requirements related to land use, water management, and waste disposal. These laws aim to mitigate the ecological footprint of mining activities, addressing issues like deforestation, soil erosion, and water pollution, which can arise from improper mining practices. By enforcing these regulations, governments seek to promote sustainable mining practices that minimize harm to the environment while maximizing economic benefits.

Taxation and Royalties
Another critical aspect of government regulation involves the financial frameworks governing gold mining. Governments often impose taxes and royalties on gold production, ensuring that a portion of the wealth generated from mining activities benefits the broader society. These financial contributions can be vital for funding public services, infrastructure projects, and community development initiatives, particularly in regions heavily impacted by mining.

Taxation policies can vary widely from country to country, with some nations offering attractive fiscal incentives to attract foreign investment, while others may have higher taxation rates to secure a more significant share of mining revenues. This balance is crucial; too low a tax rate may not provide sufficient funding for public services, whereas overly aggressive taxation can deter investment in the sector, ultimately stifling economic growth.

Community Engagement and Corporate Responsibility
In recent years, there has been a shift towards recognizing the importance of community engagement in gold mining activities. Governments are increasingly mandating that mining companies engage with local communities to address their concerns and ensure that they benefit from mining operations. This engagement can take many forms, from public consultations to the establishment of benefits-sharing agreements, where a portion of mining revenues is allocated to local development projects.

Moreover, the concept of corporate social responsibility (CSR) has gained traction, with governments encouraging or requiring mining companies to adopt ethical practices that consider the social and environmental impacts of their operations. By promoting CSR, governments aim to foster a sense of trust between mining companies and local communities, ultimately leading to more sustainable and equitable mining practices.

Addressing Illegal Mining and Artisanal Mining
Governments also face the challenge of regulating illegal and artisanal gold mining, which can lead to significant environmental damage and undermine legal mining operations. Illegal mining often occurs in remote areas where enforcement of regulations is weak, posing risks to both the environment and the health of miners. To combat this, some governments have initiated programs to formalize artisanal mining, providing training, resources, and legal frameworks that allow small-scale miners to operate responsibly within the law.

Conclusion
In summary, the role of governments in regulating gold mining is multifaceted and essential in shaping the industry's future. Through the establishment of legislative frameworks, taxation policies, community engagement, and efforts to combat illegal mining, governments can foster a mining sector that not only contributes to economic growth but also prioritizes environmental sustainability and social equity. As global demand for gold continues, the effectiveness of these regulations will be crucial in ensuring that mining practices evolve to meet the challenges of the 21st century, balancing the pursuit of wealth with the stewardship of our planet.

Gold Recycling: The Environmental Benefits
Gold recycling is increasingly recognized as a crucial component of the modern gold industry, offering significant environmental benefits that address the ecological challenges posed by traditional gold mining. As global demand for gold continues to rise, the need for sustainable practices has never been more urgent. Gold recycling provides an effective solution to mitigate the environmental impact associated with mining and extraction processes.

The Environmental Impact of Traditional Gold Mining
Traditional gold mining is notorious for its detrimental effects on the environment. It often involves large-scale excavation, which can lead to habitat destruction, soil erosion, and water pollution. The use of toxic chemicals, such as cyanide and mercury, in the extraction process poses significant risks to both ecosystems and human health. Furthermore, gold mining operations can generate substantial amounts of waste, leading to long-term contamination of land and water sources. As environmental regulations tighten and public awareness grows, the gold industry faces increasing pressure to adopt more sustainable practices.

The Role of Gold Recycling
Gold recycling, also known as gold recovery, refers to the process of reclaiming gold from various sources, including old jewelry, electronic waste, and industrial scrap. This method recycles gold that has already been mined, thereby reducing the need for new extraction and minimizing the associated environmental damage. The recycling process involves several steps, including

collection, sorting, refining, and recovery, ultimately yielding high-purity gold that can re-enter the market.

Environmental Benefits of Gold Recycling

1. Reduced Resource Depletion: By recycling gold, we can significantly decrease the demand for newly mined gold. This conserves natural resources and allows existing gold stocks to be utilized more efficiently. For instance, recycling just one ton of electronic waste can yield as much as 300 grams of gold, which is substantially higher than what can be extracted from traditional mining methods.

2. Lower Energy Consumption: The energy requirements for recycling gold are generally much lower than those for mining new gold. A study by the World Gold Council indicates that recycling gold can use up to 90% less energy compared to traditional mining. This reduction in energy consumption not only lowers greenhouse gas emissions but also helps in conserving fossil fuels.

3. Waste Minimization: Gold recycling helps reduce the volume of waste generated from mining operations. Since gold can be found in various materials, including obsolete electronics, recycling allows for the repurposing of these items instead of sending them to landfills, where they can contribute to soil and water pollution.

4. Cleaner Production Processes: The process of recycling gold typically employs cleaner technologies and methods compared to the chemical-intensive processes used in mining. Modern recycling facilities often utilize advanced techniques that minimize the release of harmful substances into the environment, making gold recovery a more eco-friendly option.

5. Economic Incentives: As the market for recycled gold expands, it creates economic opportunities within the recycling industry. This not only supports local economies but also encourages innovation in recycling technologies and processes. By promoting a circular economy, gold recycling fosters sustainability and resilience in the gold supply chain.

Conclusion
As society increasingly values sustainability, gold recycling is becoming a cornerstone of the gold industry. It offers a practical and environmentally friendly alternative to traditional gold mining, addressing the urgent need for responsible resource management. By minimizing resource depletion, reducing energy consumption, and lessening waste production, gold recycling not only benefits the environment but also promotes economic resilience. The

transition toward a more sustainable gold industry reflects a broader commitment to environmental stewardship, making gold recycling an essential practice for the future.

Community-Led Mining Initiatives: A Sustainable Approach

In recent years, the global approach to mining, particularly gold mining, has shifted towards sustainability, with communities increasingly taking the lead in these initiatives. Community-led mining initiatives are centered around local empowerment, sustainable practices, and the equitable sharing of resources. These initiatives are crucial for addressing the environmental, social, and economic challenges associated with traditional mining practices, which have historically led to ecological degradation and social injustices.

Empowering Local Communities

At the heart of community-led mining initiatives is the notion of empowerment. Local communities are often best positioned to understand their environments and the implications of mining activities. By involving community members in decision-making processes, these initiatives foster a sense of ownership and responsibility. Numerous case studies have demonstrated that when local populations are actively engaged in mining operations, they are more likely to implement practices that prioritize environmental sustainability and social equity.

For example, in parts of Africa and South America, artisanal and small-scale mining (ASM) cooperatives have emerged. These cooperatives are typically formed by local miners who pool resources and share knowledge. By organizing themselves, communities can negotiate better prices, access more sustainable mining technologies, and advocate for their rights. Moreover, these cooperatives often have strict guidelines for environmental stewardship, which helps minimize the ecological impact of their activities.

Sustainable Practices

Community-led mining initiatives often prioritize sustainability in various forms. This includes the adoption of eco-friendly extraction techniques, reduced chemical usage, and the restoration of mined lands. Many local miners are turning towards traditional methods that have less environmental impact compared to industrial-scale mining. For instance, some communities are employing gravity-based methods to extract gold, which do not involve toxic chemicals like mercury and cyanide.

Additionally, these initiatives emphasize the importance of biodiversity conservation. Local communities are more likely to value their natural surroundings and may integrate conservation efforts into their mining practices. This approach not only protects ecosystems but also ensures that communities can continue to rely on their natural resources for agriculture and other livelihoods.

Economic Benefits and Fair Trade

One of the key advantages of community-led mining initiatives is the potential for enhanced economic benefits for local populations. Instead of profits being siphoned off by multinational corporations, community-led efforts can ensure that a more significant portion of the revenue remains within the local economy. This can result in improved infrastructure, education, and health services, ultimately raising the standard of living for community members.

Furthermore, many of these initiatives are aligned with fair trade principles, ensuring that miners receive a fair price for their gold. By creating direct trade links with ethical buyers, communities can bypass exploitative middlemen and ensure that their labor is fairly compensated. This not only supports local economies but also encourages responsible consumer behavior, as buyers increasingly seek ethically sourced gold.

Challenges and Support

While community-led mining initiatives present a promising path towards sustainable gold mining, they are not without challenges. Issues such as regulatory restrictions, lack of access to financial resources, and external pressures from larger mining interests can hinder their effectiveness. Support from governments, NGOs, and international organizations can be instrumental in overcoming these challenges. Providing technical assistance, facilitating access to sustainable technologies, and advocating for fair regulations are essential steps to ensure the success of these initiatives.

In conclusion, community-led mining initiatives represent a transformative approach to gold mining, emphasizing sustainability, empowerment, and economic equity. By placing local communities at the forefront of mining practices, we can foster a more responsible and sustainable gold industry that respects both people and the planet. As these initiatives gain traction globally, they offer a hopeful vision for the future of gold mining—one that aligns with the values of social justice and environmental stewardship.

Chapter 20

Conclusion

Gold's Role in Human History: A Summary

Gold has long held a unique and multifaceted place in human history, transcending mere material value to become a symbol of wealth, power, and divine favor across various cultures and epochs. From its geological origins to its current status as a global commodity, gold's narrative is woven into the fabric of humanity, shaping economies, cultures, and societies.

The story of gold begins with its formation in the Earth's crust through geological processes, a natural phenomenon that laid the foundation for its eventual discovery by early humans. Archaeological evidence suggests that gold was one of the first metals to be utilized by prehistoric societies, not only for its aesthetic appeal but also for its malleability and resistance to tarnish. Early civilizations, such as those in Mesopotamia and Egypt, recognized gold's intrinsic qualities, leading to its use in a variety of applications ranging from tools to religious artifacts.

In ancient Egypt, gold became synonymous with the divine and the afterlife, as it was used to adorn the tombs of pharaohs and create intricate jewelry that symbolized eternal life and power. The Egyptians mined gold extensively, establishing a culture that revered the metal as a gift from the gods. This reverence was echoed in other ancient cultures, including the Indus Valley and China, where gold was integrated into trade, currency, and artistic expression. Gold facilitated commerce and cultural exchange, influencing the development of economies and social hierarchies.

As civilizations progressed, gold continued to play a pivotal role in shaping political landscapes. In ancient Greece, it was tied to myths and deities, while in the Roman Empire, gold represented wealth and authority, often used to finance military conquests and sustain imperial power. The Silk Road further expanded gold's influence, facilitating trade across continents and blending cultures in a shared appreciation for the precious metal.

The Middle Ages marked another critical chapter in gold's history, as it became a cornerstone of medieval economies and politics. The Byzantine Empire preserved and transformed traditions of gold usage, while the Islamic Golden Age saw advancements in science and trade that highlighted gold's significance in the global economy. Meanwhile, the African Kingdoms of Mali and Ghana showcased the wealth generated from gold resources, influencing trade routes and intercontinental relations.

The Age of Exploration ignited a fervent quest for gold, driving European powers to colonize new lands. The New World became synonymous with gold, leading to devastating impacts on indigenous populations and cultures. Gold rushes in California and Australia further exemplified the metal's role in shaping modern economies and societal structures, igniting waves of migration and economic booms, while also bringing to light the ethical complexities associated with gold mining.

In the contemporary era, gold's role has evolved, particularly within financial systems. The establishment of the gold standard laid the groundwork for modern monetary systems, while gold reserves became critical to national security and economic stability. The metal continues to be viewed as a safe haven in times of economic uncertainty, reflecting its enduring appeal as a store of value.

Gold's influence extends beyond economics into culture and society, symbolizing status and aspiration through jewelry, art, and popular media. It has inspired myths and legends, cementing its place in human imagination and aspiration. As we look to the future, gold's role may shift alongside technological advancements and changing societal values, yet its significance remains deeply embedded in our history.

In conclusion, gold's multifaceted role in human history encapsulates its influence across various eras and cultures, serving as a testament to humanity's complex relationship with this precious metal. From ancient rituals to modern economies, gold continues to captivate and reflect the values, aspirations, and challenges of civilizations throughout time.

The Cultural and Economic Significance of Gold

Gold has played an integral role in shaping human culture and economies throughout history, transcending its physical properties to become a powerful symbol of wealth, status, and divine favor. Its unique qualities—such as malleability, resistance to tarnish, and lustrous appearance—have made gold an ideal medium for crafting jewelry, ceremonial artifacts, and currency. This multifaceted metal has not only influenced material culture but has also left a profound imprint on social structures, trade practices, and religious beliefs.

Cultural Significance

From the dawn of civilization, gold has been intertwined with human identity and cultural expression. In ancient Egypt, gold was more than just a precious metal; it was considered the flesh of the gods and a material associated with immortality. Pharaohs adorned themselves with gold jewelry, and tombs were filled with gold artifacts to ensure a prosperous afterlife. The glimmer of gold in religious contexts also signifies divine approval and power, as seen in various cultures worldwide.

In ancient Greece, gold was not only a symbol of wealth but also a medium for artistic expression. Artists crafted intricate gold jewelry and coins that featured depictions of gods and heroes, intertwining art with mythology. The Greeks associated gold with the divine, and it played a crucial role in their rituals and temples, reinforcing its status as a symbol of power and prestige.

As cultures evolved, so did the ways in which gold was utilized and perceived. In many societies, gold became a marker of social stratification. Wealthy elites used gold to distinguish themselves from the lower classes, leading to a perception of gold as a status symbol. This association persists in modern times, where gold jewelry and ornaments often signify affluence, success, and social standing.

Economic Significance

Economically, gold has historically served as a foundation for various monetary systems. Its intrinsic value, rarity, and durability made it a trusted medium of exchange, leading to the establishment of gold as a standard for currency in many civilizations. The introduction of gold coins facilitated trade by providing a consistent value, allowing for easier exchange of goods and services.

During the Middle Ages, the expansion of gold mining and trade enriched empires and fueled economic growth. Gold became central to colonial economies, where European powers exploited gold resources in the Americas, Africa, and Asia. The influx of gold from these regions led to significant economic shifts, influencing global trade routes and prompting the rise of banking systems. Gold reserves became a benchmark for national wealth and stability, enforcing its role in international finance and diplomacy.

The establishment of the gold standard in the 19th century further cemented gold's significance in global economics. Countries pegged their currencies to gold, leading to a regulated system that stabilized international trade and investment. However, this reliance on gold also made economies vulnerable to fluctuations in gold supply and demand, prompting debates about the sustainability of gold-backed currencies.

As the world transitioned to fiat currency systems in the 20th century, the role of gold shifted yet remained vital. Gold is often viewed as a "safe haven" asset during economic uncertainty, serving as a hedge against inflation and currency devaluation. Investors turn to gold during financial crises, reinforcing its position as a reliable store of value.

Conclusion
The cultural and economic significance of gold is profound and enduring. This precious metal has shaped the course of human history, influencing social structures, artistic expression, and economic systems. Its allure transcends generations, embodying the complex interplay between wealth, power, and identity. As societies continue to evolve, gold's role as a cultural icon and economic asset will likely persist, reflecting humanity's enduring fascination with this timeless element.

Gold and Human Identity: Wealth, Power, and Perception
Gold has transcended its basic function as a precious metal to become a powerful symbol intimately woven into the fabric of human identity, wealth, and power. Throughout history, the allure of gold has shaped social hierarchies, influenced cultural narratives, and established parameters for personal and collective identity. Its unique properties—durability, malleability, and luster—have made it not only a desirable commodity for trade but also a potent emblem of status and prestige.

From ancient civilizations to modern society, gold has been at the center of wealth accumulation. In cultures across the globe, the possession of gold has signified prosperity and success. For instance, ancient Egyptians buried their pharaohs with gold artifacts, believing that these treasures would accompany them into the afterlife, thereby reinforcing the idea that gold is synonymous with enduring value. Similarly, during the Gold Rush era, individuals embarked on perilous journeys, driven by the belief that gold would secure their fortunes and elevate their social standing. The quest for gold, therefore, has often been framed as a quest for identity—where the accumulation of wealth through gold becomes a pathway to recognition and respect within one's community.

Gold's role in shaping perceptions of power is equally profound. Monarchs and leaders throughout history have adorned themselves and their palaces with gold, utilizing its gleam to project authority and divinity. The golden crowns of European monarchs or the opulent use of gold in Byzantine churches served to communicate the power and sanctity of their rulers. In these contexts, gold transcends mere materialism; it becomes a visual representation of the divine right to rule. This intertwining of gold with power dynamics is not only historical but continues in contemporary contexts, where the wealth represented by gold still influences social and political structures.

Moreover, the perception of gold is not universally positive; it has also been associated with greed, exploitation, and inequality. The historical context of gold mining often reveals stark realities, such as colonial exploitation and environmental degradation. The pursuit of gold has led to the displacement of indigenous populations and the perpetuation of socioeconomic disparities. Thus, while gold can symbolize wealth and success, it can also highlight the darker aspects of human ambition and social stratification. The duality of gold—as both a symbol of aspiration and a tool of oppression—complicates its role in shaping human identity.

In contemporary society, gold continues to influence perceptions of wealth and power, albeit in more nuanced ways. The rise of digital currencies and alternative investments has sparked debates about the future of gold as a store of value. Yet, despite these developments, gold remains a benchmark for security and stability in financial markets. Its resilience during economic downturns reinforces its status as a 'safe haven' asset, perpetuating its image as a reliable means of preserving wealth. As investors navigate an increasingly volatile economic landscape, gold's historical legacy as a symbol of wealth and power remains relevant.

Ultimately, gold's enduring allure lies in its ability to encapsulate complex human emotions and aspirations. It represents not only material wealth but also the identity and values that societies associate with economic success and personal achievement. The narratives surrounding gold, from ancient civilizations to modern economies, illustrate its profound impact on our understanding of wealth, power, and the very essence of human identity. As we continue to navigate the evolving landscape of value and currency, the significance of gold—both as a physical commodity and an enduring symbol—remains a cornerstone in the exploration of what it means to be human.

The Future of Gold in the 21st Century

As we navigate through the complexities of the 21st century, gold continues to hold a prominent place in both the global economy and cultural consciousness. While its roles have evolved—transitioning from a primary monetary standard to a multifaceted asset—gold remains an enduring symbol of value, security, and wealth. The future of gold is shaped by several interrelated trends, including technological advancements, shifting economic landscapes, changing consumer preferences, and evolving geopolitical dynamics.

Technological Innovations

One of the most significant drivers of gold's future lies in technological advancement. Innovations in mining and extraction technologies promise to enhance efficiency and sustainability in gold production. For instance, advanced techniques such as bioleaching and hydrometallurgy are being explored to minimize environmental impact while maximizing yield. Additionally, the rise of artificial intelligence (AI) and big data analytics in exploration can revolutionize how we discover new gold deposits, making it possible to identify previously inaccessible resources and optimize mining operations.

Furthermore, gold's unique properties make it invaluable in modern technology. Its exceptional conductivity and resistance to corrosion ensure its continued use in electronics, from smartphones to advanced computing systems. As technology progresses, gold is increasingly integrated into emerging fields such as nanotechnology and renewable energy solutions, particularly in photovoltaic cells and catalysts for clean energy production.

Economic Dynamics

The global economic landscape also plays a crucial role in shaping the future of gold. As central banks around the world respond to fluctuating economic conditions, gold remains a critical asset for hedging against inflation and currency devaluation. It is often seen as a "safe haven" during economic uncertainty, and its demand tends to rise in times of geopolitical tension or financial instability. The ongoing fluctuations in global markets suggest that gold will continue to be a key player in investment portfolios, especially as investors seek tangible assets that can retain value.

Moreover, the potential for a new gold standard remains a topic of discussion among economists. While the likelihood of a full return to a gold-backed currency is low, the idea of incorporating gold into modern monetary systems as a stabilizing asset is gaining traction. This could lead to an increased demand for gold, reinforcing its position as a foundational element in global finance.

Cultural Shifts

Cultural perceptions of gold are also shifting. In many societies, gold symbolizes not only wealth but also sustainability and ethical sourcing. Increasingly, consumers are conscious of the environmental and social implications of gold mining. This awareness has sparked a demand for responsibly sourced gold, leading to initiatives that emphasize ethical mining practices and transparent supply chains. The rise of certifications and standards for ethically sourced gold is likely to reshape the market, as consumers prioritize sustainability alongside traditional notions of luxury and status.

Geopolitical Factors

Geopolitical tensions and trade relations have historically influenced the value and demand for gold. As nations grapple with economic sanctions, trade wars, and shifting alliances, gold may serve as a tool for financial diplomacy. Countries may bolster their gold reserves to secure their economies against external shocks, further solidifying gold's role as a strategic asset on the global stage.

Conclusion

In conclusion, the future of gold in the 21st century is characterized by a complex interplay of technological advancements, economic volatility, cultural shifts, and geopolitical dynamics. As a multifaceted asset, gold is likely to maintain its significance not only as a store of value but also as an integral component of modern technology and sustainable practices. Its allure endures, reminding us that gold's intrinsic qualities will continue to captivate humanity, ensuring its place in our collective future. Whether viewed through the lens of investment, technology, culture, or geopolitics, gold remains a timeless element of human identity and aspiration.

Final Thoughts: The Timeless Allure of Gold

Throughout history, gold has captivated humanity with its shimmering beauty, intrinsic value, and multifaceted significance. From the earliest civilizations to the modern era, gold has transcended mere material wealth to become a symbol of power, spirituality, and cultural identity. Its allure stems from a combination of physical properties, historical associations, and psychological factors that continue to resonate across time and space.

One of the most compelling aspects of gold is its unique physical characteristics. Gold's rarity, malleability, and resistance to tarnish and corrosion have made it not only a coveted resource but also an ideal medium for crafting jewelry, coins, and artifacts. Its lustrous appearance has inspired countless artistic expressions, from intricate jewelry designs to grandiose sculptures and religious icons. The visual appeal of gold has played a vital role in shaping cultural aesthetics, making it a timeless element in art and decoration.

Moreover, gold's historical significance cannot be overstated. As one of the first metals to be widely used by humans, it has been integral to the development of economies and trade systems. The use of gold as currency and a store of value has allowed civilizations to establish complex economic structures, facilitating trade and commerce. In ancient societies, gold was often associated with the divine, linking it to gods and rulers, and thus reinforcing its status as a symbol of power and authority. This deep-rooted connection between gold and governance has persisted, influencing modern perceptions of wealth and economic stability.

Psychologically, gold holds a powerful place in human consciousness. It is often seen as a universal symbol of wealth, success, and achievement. The desire for gold can be traced back to basic human instincts, where it represents security and prosperity. This intrinsic allure is further amplified in times of economic uncertainty, where gold is perceived as a safe haven investment. During financial crises, investors flock to gold, reinforcing its status as a reliable asset. This cyclical nature of demand highlights how gold's value is not solely determined by market forces but also by cultural narratives and emotional ties.

The cultural significance of gold is perhaps most vividly illustrated in its role in rituals and traditions. Across various societies, gold has been integrated into significant life events, such as weddings, births, and funerals, symbolizing prosperity, continuity, and the passage of time. The rituals surrounding gold often elevate it beyond material possession, embedding it with meaning that transcends its physical form. This spiritual aspect of gold enriches its allure, making it a vessel of cultural heritage and collective memory.

As we look to the future, the allure of gold is unlikely to diminish. Despite technological advancements and the rise of digital assets, gold continues to hold a unique position in global finance and culture. Its historical legacy, combined with its ongoing role in modern economies, positions gold as a pivotal element of human society. As new generations engage with gold, whether through investment, fashion, or art, its significance will evolve, reflecting contemporary values and aspirations.

In conclusion, the timeless allure of gold is a multifaceted phenomenon rooted in its physical properties, historical significance, psychological appeal, and cultural importance. As humanity navigates an ever-changing world, gold remains a steadfast symbol of beauty, wealth, and power—a testament to its enduring legacy and a reminder of our shared human experience. The quest for gold, both literally and metaphorically, embodies the hopes and dreams of countless individuals and societies, ensuring that its allure will persist for generations to come.

Made in the USA
Monee, IL
21 December 2024

75016626R00094